CAREC Road Safety Engineering Manual 5

STAR RATINGS FOR ROAD SAFETY AUDIT

JUNE 2022

Contents

Tables, Figures, and Boxes

TABLES

FIGURES

BOXES

Acknowledgments

This manual was prepared under a technical assistance grant for Enhancing Road Safety for Central Asia Regional Economic Cooperation (CAREC) Member Countries (Phase 2) from the Asian Development Bank (ADB). The production of this manual was administered and managed by the CAREC Secretariat at ADB, which includes Ritu Mishra and Rebecca Stapleton.

The principal authors of this manual are Greg Smith, Kenn Beer, Luke Rogers, and Tana Tan.

The authors acknowledge the contribution of road safety audit, International Road Assessment Programme, and road safety experts from around the world in the preparation of this manual.

Abbreviations

ADB	–	Asian Development Bank
CAREC	–	Central Asia Regional Economic Cooperation
iRAP	–	International Road Assessment Programme
RSA	–	road safety audit
RSE	–	road safety engineering
SRS	–	Star rating score
SR4D	–	Star Rating for Design
SRIP	–	Safer Roads Investment Plan
SR4RSA	–	Star Ratings for Road Safety Audit

Summary

Road safety audits (RSAs) and the International Road Assessment Programme (iRAP) methodology have a common objective, to reduce road trauma, yet the two approaches are different. RSAs are a formal, systematic, and detailed examination of road safety concerns by an independent and qualified team of auditors. RSAs leverage the knowledge and experience of these auditors and only present issues the auditors believe present risks to the traveling public. The iRAP methodology is a highly standardized, data- and evidence-driven process that produces quantifiable safety metrics such as Star Ratings and investment plans.

Each of the RSA and the iRAP methodology has its own strengths and limitations; however, by combining the two, the potential of each can be amplified, and their limitations are minimized. Throughout this manual, the approach of combining RSA and the iRAP methodology is referred to as Star Ratings for Road Safety Audits (SR4RSA).

The main advantages of the SR4RSA process include the following:

(i)   Harnesses the expert experience and independence of road safety auditors but frames each audit finding within a data- and evidence-driven global standard.
(ii)   Produces objective risk metrics (Star rating scores and Star Ratings), estimates fatalities and serious injuries, and assists in achieving (and quantifying) global Star Rating targets.
(iii)   Can produce economic analysis for safety countermeasure and/or recommendation options.
(iv)   Can be a relatively easy to learn process and includes components that are highly repeatable between auditors.
(v)   Has no limit to the types and details of road safety issues that can be considered and can be context-sensitive.
(vi)   Can be performed at all stages of design, build, and pre-opening phases of a road project.
(vii)   Ensures vulnerable road users (pedestrians, cyclists, and motorcyclists) are specifically considered in the audit process, along with passenger vehicle occupants and any other road user identified by the auditors.

A core component of an SR4RSA assessment is the addition of Star Ratings for each safety concern identified and recommendation made by the RSA team. These are added for both the existing design (i.e., the design without any recommendations being implemented) and for the design with recommendations implemented. This provides the client, design team, and audit team with an evidence-based safety assessment and a measurement of the likely impact of recommendations.

This *CAREC Road Safety Engineering Manual 5: Star Ratings for Road Safety Audit* presents three approaches how the RSA and iRAP methodology can be applied together during the design phases of a road project. The three fundamental approaches for SR4RSA are as follows:

(i)   **Level 1.** This is the simplest approach and involves producing Star Ratings associated with each of the specific safety concerns and recommendations identified in the RSA. This approach makes use of the Star Rating Demonstrator, which can be used to prepare Star Ratings very quickly.
(ii)   **Level 2.** This approach adds production of Star Ratings for the length of the design, with and without the RSA recommendations. This approach makes use of the Star Rating for Design web application.
(iii)   **Level 3.** This approach adds production of Star Ratings, fatality and serious injury estimations, and investment plans for the length of the design, with and without the RSA recommendations. This approach makes use of the Star Rating for Design web application.

The decision on which approach is most suitable may depend on several factors. When a safety performance target for the design has been set, then an approach that is able to measure the performance of the design against the target should be selected. In addition to meeting the set target, the complexity of the design, time constraints, and cost may be considered when deciding on which approach should be used. In practice, elements of the three approaches can also be combined to meet specific requirements of a project. For example, a Level 2 SR4RSA could also incorporate fatality and serious injury estimations, which are part of the Level 3 approach.

This manual also introduces the concept of *situational scrutiny*, which refers to the process of bringing RSA knowledge and experience to the application of the iRAP methodology. RSA thinking can assist in improving the quality of the iRAP data inputs and interpretation, and thus the quality of the outputs, to help ensure that the full safety impacts of designs are understood and well communicated.

This manual and the tools described herein that enable the application of RSA and iRAP methodology in SR4RSA are available for everyone to use free of charge.

I. Purpose of This Manual

This *CAREC Road Safety Engineering Manual 5: Star Ratings for Road Safety Audit* (the manual) shows policy makers and practitioners how to use road safety audits (RSA) and the International Road Assessment Programme (iRAP) methodology together to produce Star Ratings for Road Safety Audits (SR4RSA). The SR4SA will help meet safety targets and improve safety in designs for new roads, road upgrades, and road rehabilitation projects.

Road crashes kill more than 1.35 million people and as many as 50 million people are injured each year, with 90% of those casualties occurring in developing countries. Road crashes are the leading cause of death around the world for children and young people between 15 and 29 years of age.[1] According to the Central Asia Regional Economic Cooperation (CAREC), road crashes are ranked as the eighth-leading cause of death globally, and sixth in Central Asia. The rate of road traffic deaths in Central and West Asian countries is between 10 to 25 per 100,000 population, which is higher compared to best-performing countries such as Sweden and the United Kingdom.[2]

In 2020, the United Nations General Assembly adopted the Stockholm Declaration and declared 2021–2030 as the second decade of action for road safety with a target of halving road deaths and injuries.[3] Reflecting evidence that the use of quantitative targets is associated with improved safety performance, the Decade of Action for Road Safety 2021–2030 (the Global Plan) recommends that national and local governments "Undertake road safety audits on all sections of new roads (pre-feasibility through to detailed design) and complete assessments using independent and accredited experts to ensure a minimum standard of three stars or better for all road users."[4] The Global Plan also emphasizes the importance of the global road safety performance targets agreed by member states, including the following:

> Target 3: "By 2030, all new roads achieve technical standards for all road users that take into account road safety, or meet a 3-Star rating or better."

> Target 4: "By 2030, more than 75% of travel on existing roads is on roads that meet technical standards for all road users that take into account road safety."[5]

The CAREC countries committed to road safety at the 14th CAREC Ministerial Conference in Mongolia in September 2015. The CAREC Road Safety Strategy 2017–2030 was endorsed by ministers from all CAREC countries during the 15th Ministerial Conference in October 2016 in Pakistan. The strategy supports and encourages governments and road authorities to plan, design, construct, and maintain roads with road safety as a key and specific objective. Among others, CAREC members endorsed RSAs as an integral part of the planning, design, and construction of road projects within the CAREC Program.

To successfully implement the Global Plan and CAREC strategy, it is valuable if policy makers, road authorities, engineers, and other key stakeholders understand how the iRAP methodology, including Star Rating performance targets, can be integrated with RSA to enhance the safety of road designs.

---

[1]   United Nations General Assembly. 2020. *Improving Global Road Safety.* New York.

[2]   Central Asia Regional Economic Cooperation (CAREC). 2017. Safely Connected: A Regional Road Safety Strategy for CAREC Countries, 2017–2030. Manila.

[3]   World Health Organization (WHO). 2020. Decade of Action for Road Safety 2021–2030 (accessed 14 September 2020).

[4]   WHO. 2021. Global Plan for the Decade of Action for Road Safety 2021–2030 (accessed 18 October 2021).

[5]   According to technical guidance published by WHO, this may be measured as a "percentage of travel that is on existing roads that meet a 3-Star rating or better for all road users." WHO. 2017. Global Road Safety Performance Targets; and W. Van den Berghe, J. J. Fleiter, and D. Cliff. 2020. *Towards the 12 Voluntary Global Targets for Road Safety. Guidance for Countries on Activities and Measures to Achieve the Voluntary Global Road Safety Performance Targets.* Brussels. p. 26.

The RSA and the iRAP methodology have the same objective: to reduce the risk of crashes occurring and to minimize the severity of crashes that do occur. However, the two approaches are different: RSA leverage the knowledge and experience of auditors while the iRAP methodology is highly standardized, driven by data and evidence, and produces quantifiable safety metrics; meaning, prior to committing to a design, it is possible to check that the scheme would in fact achieve a safety target. Each approach when used in isolation holds potential to improve safety; nevertheless, according to the Permanent International Association of Road Congresses, infrastructure safety management tools such as RSA and the iRAP methodology can (and should) be used in parallel exactly because of the different but complementary perspectives they bring to the road design process.[6]

The purpose of this manual is, therefore, to share approaches for how policy makers and practitioners can use RSA and the iRAP methodology together to improve safety in road designs and achieve safety performance targets for new roads, road upgrades, and road rehabilitation projects. Throughout this manual, the approach of combining RSA and the iRAP methodology is referred to as Star Ratings for Road Safety Audits (SR4RSA).

This manual is not designed to teach people how to perform RSA or use the iRAP methodology as each of these require specific training and experience. Rather, the focus is to explain how the two processes can be combined. Nonetheless, this manual does provide worked examples and guidance on key technical issues that may be encountered while performing a SR4RSA assessment.

The 2018 CAREC Road Safety Engineering Manual 1: Road Safety Audits (CAREC RSE Manual 1) provides guidance on the process for RSA, including why proactive approaches to road safety are valuable, who is involved in RSA, the elements of the process, and steps involved in performing and managing RSA.[7] For simplicity, the focus of this manual is on how the iRAP methodology may be integrated with the well-established RSA processes.

CAREC RSE Manual 1 identifies three main groups involved in RSA:

(i)   The client. The organization responsible for the project and which is deemed to be the owner of the road.
(ii) The design team. An individual or team commissioned by the project manager on behalf of the client to design the road project. The designer may be a part of the client organization, a design institute, or may come from a separate consulting company.
(iii) The audit team. Usually comprises at least two people who are qualified as road safety auditors, and who are independent of the design and the proposal. The audit team is engaged by the project manager for the client. While the audit team may come from the client organization (provided team members are clearly independent of the project), they are most commonly from specialist organizations and consultancy companies.

Those same groups are referred to and their roles are explained throughout this manual.

6   Permanent International Association of Road Congresses. 2019. Road Safety Manual, Management Tools (accessed 14 September 2020).
7   ADB. 2018. CAREC Road Safety Engineering Manual 1: Road Safety Audits. Manila.

A crowded avenue in Karachi where the police guards try to control the traffic (photo by jprat).

People cross the road at a pedestrian crossing in the city of Nur-Sultan (Astana) (photo by Nurlan Tastanbekov).

II.   The Safe System Approach

The Safe System approach is founded on the premise that human life and health is the priority for the road system, and this cannot be traded for mobility. The aim of the Safe System approach is to ensure that in the event of a crash, impact energies remain below the levels that cause death or serious injury. Countries leading in road safety have implemented this approach with outstanding results, and it is the foundation of the United Nations Decade of Action for Road Safety 2021–2030 (the Global Plan).[8]

The approach is based on well-established safety principles:

Mistakes, errors of judgment, and poor decisions are intrinsic to humans.

Humans are fragile. Unprotected, we cannot survive impacts that occur at greater than around 30 kilometers per hour (kph).

The "engineered" elements of the system—vehicles and roads—can be designed to be compatible with the human element, recognizing that while crashes might occur, the total system can be designed to minimize harm, particularly by making roads "self-explaining" and "forgiving" of human error.

Road safety is a shared responsibility. Those who use roads have a responsibility to act with the safety of themselves and others in mind and comply with laws. Those who design, build, maintain, and manage the roads and vehicles have a responsibility to proactively improve the safety of the entire system.

With more than 70% of the global population expected to live in urban settings by 2030, the application of the Safe System approach in villages, towns and cities is especially important. The Global Plan highlights that investment in public transport systems that facilitate safe and efficient movement of large and growing populations, and in the healthiest and cleanest modes of transport—walking and cycling—will be central to safely meeting increased demand for urban mobility.[9] Ensuring that road designs are fundamentally safe for all expected modes, abilities, and journeys is essential in achieving this.

Road infrastructure management tools that support the implementation of the Safe System approach may be categorized into two groups: reactive and proactive tools. Reactive tools, such as "black spot" programs, are used to develop safety plans based on crash data that identifies where clusters of serious crashes have occurred in the past. However, these approaches rely heavily on the availability of good quality data, which are often not available.[10] Evidence also shows that over time, the proportion of serious crashes that occur at black spot locations typically decreases.[11] As such, reactive tools alone are insufficient to support a Safe System approach. Proactive tools are used to develop safety plans by focusing on fundamental flaws in roads and designs to identify where serious road crashes are likely to happen in the future. They provide a means of systematically managing risk across road networks and support the Safe System approach. Road safety audits and the iRAP methodology each offer proactive approaches for road infrastructure safety management.

---

[8]   See, for example, World Resources Institute. 2018. Sustainable and Safe: A Vision and Guidance for Zero Road Deaths. Washington, DC.

[9]   WHO. 2021. Global Plan for the Decade of Action for Road Safety 2021–2030 (accessed 18 October 2021).

[10]   Permanent International Association of Road Congresses. 2019. Road Safety Manual, Data Quality and Under-Reporting (accessed 14 September 2020).

[11]   Permanent International Association of Road Congresses. 2019. Road Safety Manual, Proactive Identification (accessed 14 September 2020).

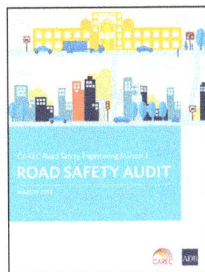

Road safety audits (RSAs) are described in detail in the *CAREC RSE Manual 1*. RSAs are a formal, systematic, and detailed examination of road safety concerns by an independent and qualified team of auditors. RSAs involve reviews of designs and inspections at locations on a new or upgraded road. They focus on identifying potential safety concerns and opportunities to eliminate or mitigate risk.

RSAs are performed by a team consisting of a team leader (a senior road safety auditor) and a team that has experience spanning road safety engineering, design, and local road user behavior.

The process of commissioning an RSA consists of the following steps:

(i)   Determine if an audit is needed.
(ii)   Select an audit team leader who then engages the audit team.
(iii) Draft the pre-audit communication to provide information (such as drawings and design reports) about the project to the team leader, outlining the project and discussing the audit ahead.
(iv)   Assess the drawings for safety issues (the "desktop" audit).
(v)   Inspect the site both during daytime and nighttime.
(vi)   Write the audit report and send to the project manager.

(vii) Discuss the key safety issues and clarify outstanding matters during post-audit communication.
(viii) Write a response report, referring to each audit recommendation.
(ix)   Follow up and implement agreed changes.

During the planning, design, and construction of a new or upgraded road or a road rehabilitation project, an RSA may be performed at several stages:

(i)   feasibility stage,
(ii)   preliminary design stage,
(iii) detailed design stage,
(iv)   road works stage,
(v)   preopening stage, and
(vi)   existing road (road safety inspections).

The *CAREC RSE Manual 1* explains that road safety inspections of existing roads are sometimes considered the sixth stage at which RSA may be useful. As is discussed in the following chapter, the iRAP methodology is used widely as a key input for road safety inspections of existing roads.

RSAs should never be seen as a check that standards have been met. Instead, RSAs should be approached as assessments of how future road users will use a new or upgraded road and whether these road users may face safety issues, whether driving, walking, or riding. In other words, the audit team's job is to put itself into the shoes of future road users and assess how safety on a new or upgraded road will work for them.

IV. What Is the International Road Assessment Programme Methodology?

The iRAP methodology was developed to accelerate the implementation of safe infrastructure globally. The iRAP methodology is internationally recognized and offers evidence-based approaches to guide planning, design, investment, and policy setting. The methodology has been used in more than 100 countries to assess more than 2 million kilometers (km) of roads and designs.

The iRAP methodology comprises several protocols. The Crash Rate Risk Mapping protocol is based on actual crash data and offers a reactive approach to risk management. Star ratings, fatality, and serious injury estimations; and Safer Roads Investment Plans (SRIPs) are part of a proactive approach to risk management; that is, like RSA they can be performed without reference to detailed crash data. These proactive approaches are the focus of this manual and, for simplicity, are referred to herein as the iRAP methodology. The iRAP methodology may be applied to existing roads and designs, both for very short lengths (down to 100 meters [m]) and for very long lengths (including entire networks), and may be used in support of road safety inspections and road safety impact assessments.

Following is the process for performing the iRAP methodology:

(i) **Data are collected about the road or design.** These data include a fixed list of 52 road infrastructure attributes that are known to have an impact on the likelihood of a crash and its severity (e.g., the presence of sidewalks, types of intersections, roadside conditions, numbers of traffic lanes, etc.); traffic speeds; and traffic flow for each 100 m of a road or design.

(ii) **These data are then combined with crash modification factors to produce Star rating scores (SRS) and Star Ratings.** Star Ratings are an international benchmark used to estimate the risk that a person—whether traveling in a vehicle, riding a motorcycle, walking, or riding a bicycle—will be killed or seriously injured. 1-Star roads and designs have the highest infrastructure-related risk, while 5-Star roads have the lowest risk (and lowest SRS).

(iii) **Estimate fatality and serious injury.** Estimations may be calculated for the road or design by drawing on the data that underpins the Star Ratings, flow (or exposure) data, and network-level crash data.

(iv) **Safer Roads Investment Plans may then be developed.** An SRIP is a prioritized list of countermeasures that could cost-effectively improve a road or its design Star Ratings to reduce infrastructure-related risk. The plans are based on an economic analysis of a range of countermeasures, undertaken by comparing the cost of implementing the countermeasure with the reduction in crash costs that would result from its implementation. The plans contain extensive planning and engineering information such as road attribute records, countermeasure options, and economic assessments for each 100 m segment of a road network.

The iRAP methodology is described in detail in fact sheets, specifications, manuals, and guides.[12] The tools that enable the application of the iRAP methodology are available for free through the online software ViDA (meaning "life" in Spanish).[13] Tools that are specifically cited in this manual are the Star Rating Demonstrator, which enables quick calculation of SRS and Star Ratings for a single road segment with virtually any combination of design attributes, and the Star Rating for Design (SR4D) application, which supports assessments along longer lengths of roads and designs. Each of these tools is described in more detail in subsequent chapters. These tools are complemented by the *Road Safety Toolkit* that offers free, practical information on the causes and prevention of serious road crashes.[14]

---

[12] iRAP. 2021. *iRAP Methodology Fact Sheets* (accessed 14 September 2021); and iRAP. 2021. *iRAP Specification, Manuals and Guides* (accessed 14 September 2021).

[13] iRAP. 2021. *Welcome to ViDA. The iRAP Online Software to Help Create a World Free of High Risk Roads* (accessed 14 September 2021).

[14] iRAP. 2021. Road Safety Toolkit (accessed 14 September 2021).

Assessments using the iRAP methodology are a highly cost-effective measure for identifying and addressing likely safety issues. It is estimated that achieving Global Road Safety Performance Target 4 whereby 75% of travel occurs on roads rated 3-Star or better for all road users would prevent more than 450,000 fatalities per year. This would generate a cost–benefit ratio of 8:1 globally and 18:1 for low-income countries, 11:1 for lower-middle income countries, 15:1 for upper middle-income countries, and 4:1 for high-income countries.[15] Projects that involve the iRAP methodology have resulted in fatality reductions of more than 40% and safety countermeasures that cost 10% or less of the road construction.[16] The cost of performing an iRAP assessment is often less than 0.1% of the cost of safety countermeasures implemented.

Assessments using the iRAP methodology are especially cost-effective on longer road or design lengths. The earlier the assessment is undertaken in a project, the greater the benefit, as adjusting design plans can be a cheaper option than retrofitting safety features once a design has been built. The methodology is also valuable for post-construction assessments, to confirm that targets have been met. Box 1 provides an example of an assessment using the iRAP methodology on a road network, illustrating the potential of ensuring that 75% of travel occurs on roads rated 3-Star or better. Worked examples involving the iRAP methodology during the design process in support of Global Road Safety Performance Target 3 are provided in Chapter 9.

Box 1: Achieving the United Nations Global Performance Target 4

The Roads Department of the Ministry of Regional Development and Infrastructure of Georgia with support of the World Bank undertook assessments using the International Road Assessment Programme (iRAP) methodology on more than 500 kilometers (km) of road in the Mtskheta–Mtianeti region. The network connects several towns and villages within and outside the region, and carries interregional as well as intraregional vehicular traffic.

The assessments showed that less than 20% of travel occurs on roads rated 3-Star or better (see Box Figure 1.1). The Roads Department examined several treatment options, including a scenario where reductions in traffic speeds on undivided urban stretches and selected rural stretches would be complemented with cost-effective infrastructure safety countermeasures. It was estimated that this scenario would reduce serious trauma by 57%, saving more than 4,000 deaths and serious injuries over 20 years. The cost–benefit ratio of the infrastructure safety countermeasures would exceed 5:1.

As the treatment program targeted risky sections of the network where most travel occurs, it was estimated that it would result in 75% of travel occurring on roads rated 3-Star or better, thereby ensuring the network meets the United Nations Global Road Safety Performance Target 4.

continued on next page

---

[15]   iRAP. 2017. The Business Case for Safer Roads (accessed 14 September 2021).

[16]   See, for example, A. Kumar, P. Tvgssshrk, and S. K. Tadimalla. 2019. Human Lives Need Not Be Lost in Road Crashes—Much Less at Current Levels. *World Bank Blogs* (accessed 14 September 2021); P. Tvgssshrk. 2018. Building Safer Roads Through Better Design and Better Contracts. *World Bank Blogs* (accessed 14 September 2021); and N. Gupta. 2018. Road Safety Action Pays Off, and "Demonstration Corridors" Are Here to Prove It. *World Bank Blogs* (accessed 14 September 2021).

Box: *continued*

Box Figure 1.1: Vehicle Occupant Star Ratings for the Existing Network (left) and with Safety Treatments to Achieve 75% of Travel on 3-Star or Better Roads (right)

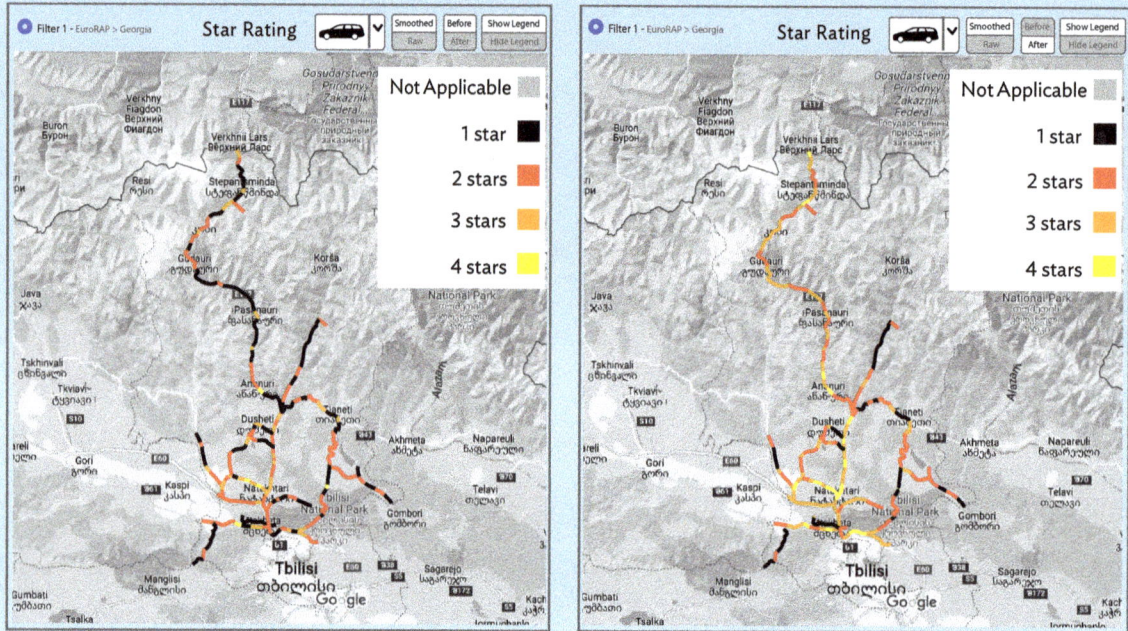

iRAP = International Road Assessment Programme.
Source: iRAP analysis from data in iRAP. 2021. *iRAP Assessment in Mtskheta–Mtianeti Region, Georgia. Final Report.* London.

V.   Why Link Road Safety Audits and the International Road Assessment Programme Methodology?

RSAs and the iRAP methodology represent different, yet complementary, approaches to road infrastructure safety management. They each have strengths and limitations; however, by combining the two, the potential of each approach can be amplified. The iRAP methodology is enhanced by the experience and expertise that road safety auditors bring to the design process and by the ability of the RSA to examine all aspects of infrastructure safety in detail. RSAs are enhanced by the ability of the iRAP methodology to produce objective and repeatable metrics, most notably Star Ratings, which provide evidence about the seriousness of safety concerns and likely impact of recommendations. Thus, it can be used to create a quantified "pass" mark for the safety of designs. Table 1 summarizes key strengths and limitations of the two approaches and provides a useful insight into the complementarity of the RSA and the iRAP methodology and therefore the potential of the Star Ratings for Road Safety Audits (SR4RSA) process.

Table 1: Relative Strengths and Limitations of Road Safety Audits and the International Road Assessment Programme Methodology

	Road Safety Audits	iRAP Methodology
Strengths	• Harnesses expert experience and independence • Relatively easy to learn process • No limit to the types of road safety issues that can be considered (e.g., self-explaining design, road user task workload) • Can be context-sensitive • No limit to the level of detail that can be considered • No limit to the types of road users that can be considered • Can be performed at all stages of design, build, and pre-opening phases of a road project • Can be performed for designs of all types of roads • Can be performed during day and night • Can consider weather-related factors such as rain, fog, snow, and ice	• Global standard and highly repeatable between users • Data- and evidence-driven for key road attributes, speed, and exposure • Major road user types: vehicle occupants, motorcyclists, pedestrians, and bicyclists • Can be applied on a 100-meter road segment or an entire road network • Able to produce objective risk metrics (Star rating scores and Star Ratings) and estimates of fatalities and serious injuries • Able to produce economic analysis for safety countermeasure options • May be performed for all types of existing roads and designs • Enables setting of quantitative safety targets • Results are available in a central web platform • Supported by a global training and accreditation scheme
Limitations	• No globally accepted standard or qualification • Dependent on the expertise of the auditors • Subjectivity can lead to inconsistencies between auditors • Can be challenging to perform detailed audits on long road lengths • The needs of vulnerable road users are sometimes inadvertently neglected • In practice, the focus can tend toward low-cost but low-impact treatments • No financial or quantified impact analysis	• Fixed list of attributes is used in the assessment • Segment lengths (inspection intervals) are fixed at 100 meters • May only be performed in daylight and does not consider weather-related factors such as rain, snow, and ice • The quality of results depends on the quality of input data • Results can be misinterpreted without expert knowledge • Relatively heavy data requirements for a full assessment

iRAP = International Road Assessment Programme.
Sources: iRAP and Safe System Solutions.

Night shot of highway highlighting "cat eyes" in Hazara Expressway, Abbottabad (photo by Obaid).

VI. Safety Performance Targets

A key strength of the iRAP methodology is that it generates metrics that can be used to establish quantitative safety targets. This means that prior to committing to a design, it is possible to check that the scheme would in fact achieve a safety target. Adjustments to the designs can then be made in places where the target is not met. Evidence indicates that this kind of use of quantitative targets is associated with improved safety performance.[17] Such targets can help to trigger new behaviors, guide focus, and help to sustain momentum and future progress. It is generally regarded that you cannot manage what you do not measure; and you cannot improve upon something that you do not properly manage.

It is the role of the client to set targets for a design and it is the responsibility of the design team to achieve them. In conjunction with RSA, audit teams may be required to check whether the design meets one or more targets and/or make recommendations about how the design can be improved to meet such targets. It is not the role of an audit team to set a target for a design, however the type of target is a factor in deciding what SR4RSA approach is appropriate. As such, it is important that the client, design team, and audit team each have an awareness of the types of targets that may be set for a design.

Targets based on the iRAP methodology are used at several levels. Internationally, they are reflected in the Global Plan and two of the 12 voluntary Global Road Safety Performance Targets:[18]

(i) The Global Plan recommends that national and local governments "Undertake road safety audits on all sections of new roads (pre-feasibility through to detailed design) and complete assessments using independent and accredited experts to ensure a minimum standard of 3-stars or better for all road users."

(ii) Global Road Safety Performance Target 3 states, "By 2030, all new roads achieve technical standards for all road users that take into account road safety, or meet a 3-Star rating or better."

(iii) Global Road Safety Performance Target 4 states, "By 2030, more than 75% of travel on existing roads is on roads that meet technical standards for all road users that take into account road safety." According to guidance published by World Health Organization, this may be measured as a "percentage of travel that is on existing roads that meet a 3-Star rating or better for all road users."

At the country level, variations on the Global Road Safety Performance Targets are used strategically for national and subnational road networks. For example, 100% of newly built national highways and provincial roads (grade III or higher) and 75% of the total length of the national highway network being exploited reach the traffic safety level of 3-Star.[19]

At the road project level, several forms of targets may be set depending on the project context and design priorities. The simplest form of target is based on Global Road Safety Performance Target 3, i.e., *"The design must achieve a minimum of 3-Star for all road users."* While targets are most often set based on Star Ratings, the iRAP methodology also enables quantitative targets to be set based on road attributes and estimated numbers of fatalities and serious injuries. These targets may be used in project management documents including in design specifications for design teams, design and monitoring frameworks, and project development objectives. Table 2 lists examples of the types of targets that may be used and encountered in a design project. In practice, elements of the targets listed in the table could also be combined. The table also includes guidance on which of the three SR4RSA approaches (described in detail in Chapter 9) may be used with each target.

---

17 OECD International Transport Forum. 2008. Towards Zero: Ambitious Road Safety Targets and the Safe System Approach. Paris.

18 WHO. 2021. Global Plan for the Decade of Action for Road Safety 2021–2030 (accessed 18 October 2021); W. Van den Berghe, J. J. Fleiter, and D. Cliff. 2020. *Towards the 12 Voluntary Global Targets for Road Safety. Guidance for Countries on Activities and Measures to Achieve the Voluntary Global Road Safety Performance Targets.* Brussels.

19 Government of the Socialist Republic of Viet Nam. 2020. *Approving the National Strategy for Ensuring Road Traffic Order and Safety for the Period 2021–2030 and a Vision to 2045.* Hanoi.

Table 2: Examples of Quantitative Safety Performance Targets That Can Be Set with the International Road Assessment Programme Methodology

Type	Example of Target[c]	SR4RSA Approach[b]
Based on global performance target 3[a]	The design must achieve a minimum of 3-Star for all road users.	Level 1 (partial) Level 2 Level 3
Improvement	The design must achieve an improvement in Star Ratings for all road users relative to the existing road.[d]	Level 1 (partial) Level 2 Level 3
Different levels of exposure	The design must achieve a minimum of 3-Star for all road users and where the design traffic flow is more than 50,000 vehicles per day, the design must achieve a minimum of 4-Star for all users.	Level 1 (partial) Level 2 Level 3
Specific road users and area type	The design must achieve a minimum of 3-Star for all road users and for sections that pass through linear settlements the design must achieve a minimum 4-Star standard for pedestrians and cyclists.	Level 1 (partial) Level 2 Level 3
Exposure and road users	The design must achieve a minimum of 3-Star for pedestrians where peak flows are greater than five people per hour.	Level 1 (partial) Level 2 Level 3
Road attributes	The design must provide sidewalks along 100% of the length, or 100% of pedestrian crossings have street lighting.	Level 2 Level 3
Fatalities and serious injuries	The estimated number of fatalities and serious injuries associated with the design must not exceed "X" per year.	Level 3
	The estimated number of fatalities and serious injuries associated with the design must be at least % lower than that of the existing road.[e]	Level 3
Relative fatality and serious injury rate estimates	The estimated number of fatalities and serious injuries per vehicle kilometer traveled must be lower than the average for the type of road.[f]	Level 3

[a] Global Road Safety Performance Target 3 states, "By 2030, all new roads achieve technical standards for all road users that take into account road safety, or meet a 3-Star rating or better." See WHO. 2021. Global Plan for the Decade of Action for Road Safety 2021–2030 (accessed 18 October 2021).

[b] The three SR4RSA approaches are (i) Level 1: involves producing Star Ratings associated with each of the specific safety concerns and recommendations identified in the RSA; (ii) Level 2: adds production of Star Ratings for the length of the design, with and without the RSA recommendations; and (iii) Level 3: adds production of Star Ratings, fatality estimations, and investment plans for the length of the design, with and without the RSA recommendations.

[c] Star Rating targets are based on *smoothed* Star Ratings. Targets also only apply to sections of the road or design where the corresponding road users are present on the road.

[d] Requires an assessment of an existing road to be performed.

[e] Requires knowledge of fatalities and serious injuries on existing roads.

[f] Requires knowledge of average fatality and serious injury rates for road type.

Source: International Road Assessment Programme (iRAP).

High-speed, wide road in Uzbekistan (photo by Armastas).

Safety must be proactively addressed at all stages of a road's life cycle, and it is the role of the client to determine which process will be applied and when they should be applied (footnote 11). The most cost-effective way to improve road safety is to include road safety design in the earliest part of a road design and life cycle.

Figure 1 illustrates the typical stages of a road's life and when RSA and the iRAP methodology may be applied. The SR4RSA process can be applied during the concept, draft, and detailed design phases.

A. Project Planning

Because of its quantifiable, segmented, and standardized approach, the iRAP methodology is highly suitable for road safety inspections to detect potential crash risks. These inspections provide detailed information that may be used to plan future road improvements, develop budgets, and set policy targets. Although RSAs (and therefore SR4RSA) are generally not performed at the project planning stage, a road safety auditor's skill can be utilized during this phase if specific elements of the assessment using the iRAP methodology require *situational scrutiny* to determine the most appropriate coding of a segment (see Chapter 10).

Figure 1: Where Road Safety Audits and International Road Assessment Programme Can Be Applied in a Road's Life Cycle

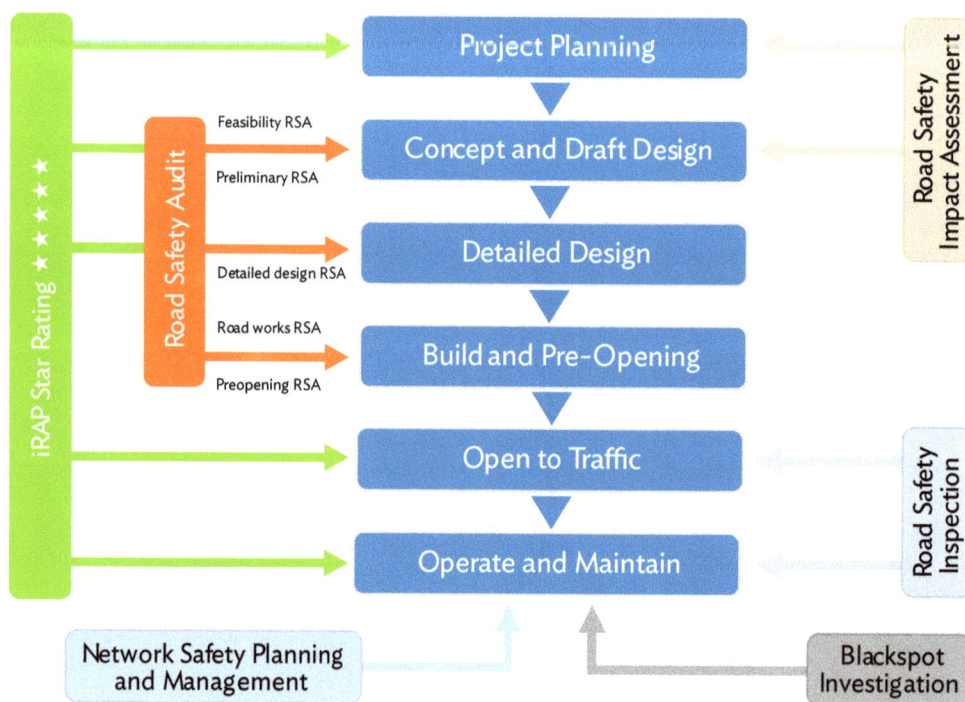

iRAP = International Road Assessment Programme, RSA = road safety audit.
Sources: International Road Assessment Programme (iRAP) and Safe System Solutions Pty Ltd.

B.   Concept and Draft Design

The potential to create a genuinely safe road environment is perhaps greatest at the concept and draft design stage of a road's life cycle. As such, making the SR4RSA process an integral part of these phases of a project is a priority. At the early concept design stage, expert advice provided during a feasibility stage RSA can be used to influence fundamental factors such as the choice of design standards, route, key cross-sections layouts, and continuity with the existing road network. The iRAP methodology may be used to support the RSA or road safety impact assessment of various design scheme options, and support decision-making about the option with the best outcome for road safety with metrics such as Star Ratings, fatality serious injury estimations, and cost estimates.[20] When a concept design has been developed, the SR4RSA process can play an important role in further shaping the draft designs; influencing factors such as alignment, intersection form, and cross section elements; and designing facilities for pedestrians, bicyclists, and motorcyclists.

C.   Detailed Design

Once the concept and draft design has been produced, the scope of the project has generally been set. The detailed design involves specification of elements such as drainage, pavement, signage, line marking, roadside barrier design, sidewalk and other paths' widths, and the specifics of any new controls. The RSA provides detailed analysis of these features to ensure they do not present an increased risk to road users and that they are being implemented in a manner that results in the greatest road safety gains. The iRAP methodology provides a way of checking the road safety impact for different features and/or alterations to the detailed design, and modelling the economic cost and benefits of the designs. Even at this detailed design, stage auditors should, where possible, refer to the original Star Rating of the concept and draft designs to ensure the road safety intent of the project is being realized.

D.   Build and Pre-Opening

The road safety of the traveling public and road workers is important during construction because of the out-of-context road environment during this period. RSAs are important at this stage and the *CAREC Road Safety Engineering Manual 2: Safer Road Works* also provides valuable guidance.[21] The SR4RSA approach will provide benefits at the pre-opening stage.

E.   Operate and Maintain

Once the road is open to traffic, the iRAP methodology may again be used for road safety inspections to confirm that the Star Rating target for the design has in fact been met and detects potential crash risks. This is typically performed 3–6 months after the road is open to traffic. A road safety auditor's skill set could assist to identify specific features that may be presenting unanticipated road safety risks by, for example, creating confusion, being misinterpreted, or being misused by road users. As the road matures, the iRAP methodology may be used to monitor safety risks over time as features such as line marking, signs, and pavement deteriorate. The surrounding land use changes, and traffic flows and speeds also change, affecting the Star Ratings.

Pedestrians crossing a road in Uzbekistan (photo by Anvar Matkarimov).

---

[20]   See footnote 21 for discussion on road safety impact assessments.

[21]   ADB. 2018. *CAREC Road Safety Engineering Manual 3: Safer Road Works.* Manila.

VIII. How Can Road Safety Audits Be Integrated with the International Road Assessment Programme Methodology?

The *CAREC Road Safety Engineering (RSE) Manual 1* describes a series of steps involved in the RSA process and the respective responsibilities. Table 3 (which presents some SR4RSA steps detailed in Chapters 8, 9, and 12) is an adaptation of the table in the *CAREC* *RSE Manual 1* and indicates how the SR4RSA process can be easily integrated into the RSA process. The additions to the table to accommodate the SR4RSA process are shown in italics.

Table 3: Key Steps in the Road Safety Audit Process with iRAP Assessments

SR4RSA Step	Responsibility
1. Determine if an audit is needed and, *if so, select the SR4RSA approach.*	Client
2. Select an audit team leader who then engages the audit team. *Consider the competencies needed within the audit team.*	Client and audit team leader
3. Draft the pre-audit communication to provide information (e.g., drawings, design reports *and any existing iRAP assessment data such as Star Ratings, fatality and serious injury estimations or investment plans, etc.*) about the project to the team leader, outlining the project and discuss the audit ahead.	Design team (via client) and audit team leader
4. Assess the drawings for safety issues (the "desktop" audit) *and perform the iRAP assessment at the desired level of detail.*	Audit team
5. Inspect the site both during daytime and nighttime and *collect data that can support an iRAP assessment.*	Audit team
6. Write the audit report *including iRAP assessment and send to the project manager.*	Audit team
7. Discuss the key safety issues and clarify outstanding matters during post-audit communication.	Client (plus design team) and audit team leader
8. Write a response report, referring to each audit recommendation.	Client
9. Follow up and implement agreed changes.	Client (and design team)

iRAP = International Road Assessment Programme, SR4RSA = Star Rating for Road Safety Audit.
Source: Adapted from Table 1 in ADB. 2018. *CAREC Road Safety Engineering Manual 1: Road Safety Audit.* Manila.

IX.   Worked Examples to Illustrate the Approaches for SR4RSA

There are numerous ways that RSA and the iRAP methodology can be applied together during the design phases of a road project. There are three fundamental approaches for SR4RSA:

(i) **Level 1:** This approach involves producing Star Ratings associated with each of the specific safety concerns and recommendations identified in the RSA.

(ii) **Level 2:** This approach adds production of Star Ratings for the length of the design, with and without the RSA recommendations.

(iii) **Level 3:** This approach adds production of Star Ratings, fatality estimations, and investment plans for the length of the design, with and without the RSA recommendations.

A core component of an SR4RSA assessment is the addition of Star Ratings for each safety concern identified and recommendation made by the RSA team. These are added for both the existing design (i.e., the design without any recommendations being implemented) and for the design with recommendations implemented (Figure 2). This provides the client, design team, and audit team with an evidence-based safety assessment and a measurement of the likely impact of recommendations.

In practice, elements of the three approaches can also be combined to meet specific requirements of a project. For example, a Level 2 SR4RSA could also

incorporate fatality and serious injury estimations, which are part of the Level 3 approach. The decision on which approach is most suitable may be guided by the client, design team, and audit team depending on the project context and design priorities. If a safety performance target for the design has been set, then an approach that is able to measure the performance of the design against the target should be selected.[22] Apart from meeting a target, the complexity of the design, time constraints, and cost may be considered when deciding on which approach should be used.

Prior to describing the three SR4RSA levels in detail, it is necessary to consider the fundamentals of the Star Ratings:[23]

(i) **Star rating scores and Star Ratings.** Star rating scores (SRS) are a unitless decimal number that underpin the Star Ratings. Star Ratings are determined by assigning SRS to the bands as shown in Figure 3. SRS provide a more precise measure of risk than the Star Ratings and so can be useful in understanding underlying changes in risk as designs are modified to reflect safety recommendations. For example, if a recommendation resulted in the SRS for bicyclists decreasing from 15.67 to 13.06, this represents a 17% reduction in risk of death or serious injury to bicyclists, but it would not result in a Star Rating change because the SRS are both within the 3-Star band (Figure 4).

---

[22] Road safety performance targets are discussed in more detail in section 13.

[23] These topics are described in more detail in iRAP. 2021. *iRAP Methodology Fact Sheets* (accessed 14 September 2021).

Figure 2: Typical Road Safety Audit Safety Concerns and Recommendations with Star Ratings

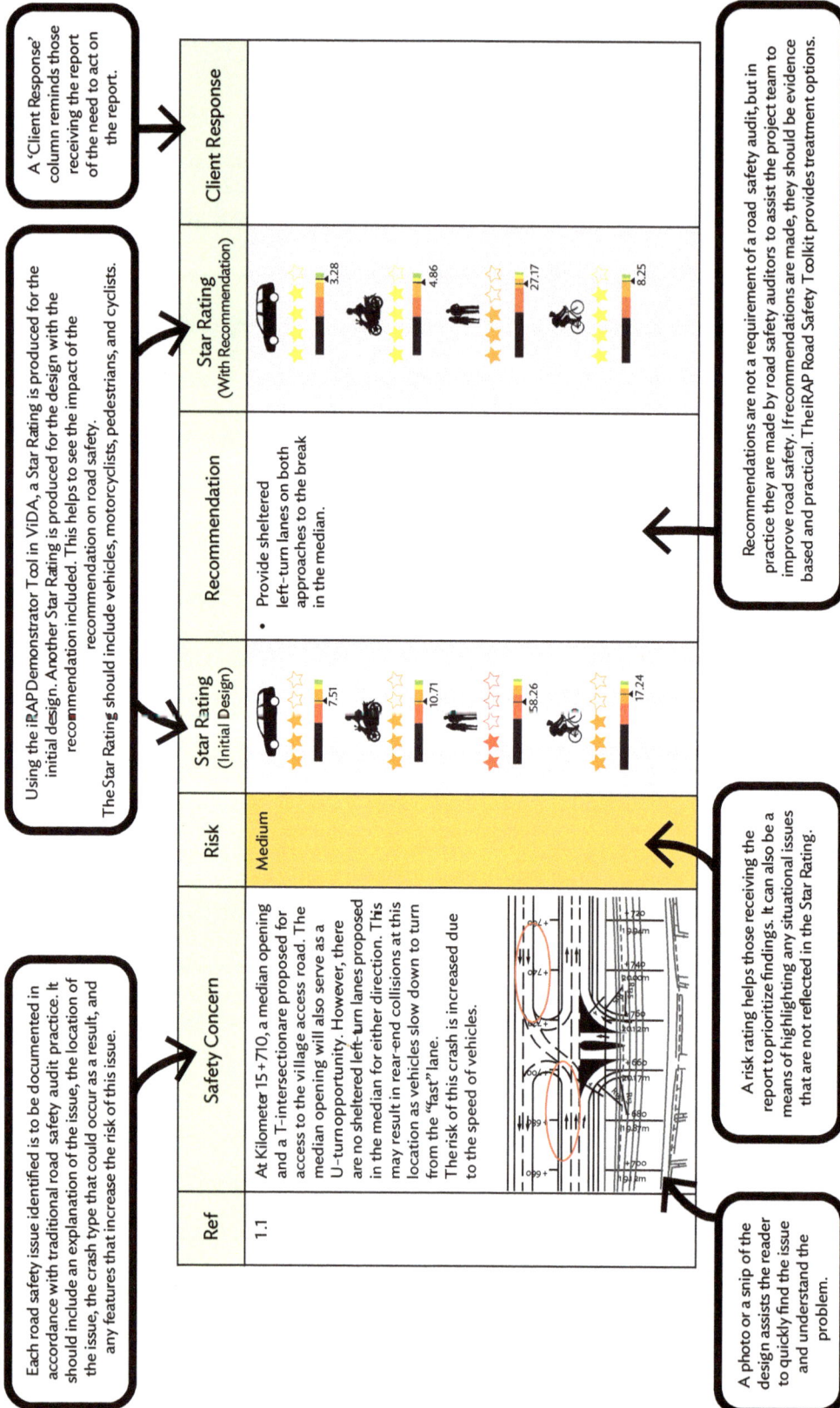

Each road safety issue identified is to be documented in accordance with traditional road safety audit practice. It should include an explanation of the issue, the location of the issue, the crash type that could occur as a result, and any features that increase the risk of this issue.

Using the iRAP Demonstrator Tool in ViDA, a Star Rating is produced for the initial design. Another Star Rating is produced for the design with the recommendation included. This helps to see the impact of the recommendation on road safety.
The Star Rating should include vehicles, motorcyclists, pedestrians, and cyclists.

A 'Client Response' column reminds those receiving the report of the need to act on the report.

Recommendations are not a requirement of a road safety audit, but in practice they are made by road safety auditors to assist the project team to improve road safety. If recommendations are made, they should be evidence based and practical. The iRAP Road Safety Toolkit provides treatment options.

A risk rating helps those receiving the report to prioritize findings. It can also be a means of highlighting any situational issues that are not reflected in the Star Rating.

A photo or a snip of the design assists the reader to quickly find the issue and understand the problem.

Ref	Safety Concern	Risk	Star Rating (Initial Design)	Recommendation	Star Rating (With Recommendation)	Client Response
1.1	At Kilometer 15+710, a median opening and a T-intersectionare proposed for access to the village access road. The median opening will also serve as a U-turn opportunity. However, there are no sheltered left-turn lanes proposed in the median for either direction. This may result in rear-end collisions at this location as vehicles slow down to turn from the "fast" lane. The risk of this crash is increased due to the speed of vehicles.	Medium	7.51 / 10.71 / 58.26 / 17.24	• Provide sheltered left-turn lanes on both approaches to the break in the median.	3.28 / 4.86 / 27.17 / 8.25	

Sources: International Road Assessment Programme (iRAP) and Safe System Solutions Pty Ltd.

Figure 3: Star Rating Bands

Star Rating	Star Rating Score				
	Vehicle occupants and motorcyclists	Bicyclists	Pedestrians		
			Total	Along	Crossing
5	0 to < 2.5	0 to < 5	0 to < 5	0 to < 0.2	0 to < 4.8
4	2.5 to < 5	5 to < 10	5 to < 15	0.2 to < 1	4.8 to < 14
3	5 to < 12.5	10 to < 30	15 to < 40	1 to < 7.5	14 to < 32.5
2	12.5 to < 22.5	30 to < 60	40 to < 90	7.5 to < 15	32.5 to < 75
1	22.5 +	60+	90 +	15 +	75 +

Note: 1-Star is highest risk and 5-Star is lowest risk.
Source: International Road Assessment Programme (iRAP). 2021. *iRAP Methodology Fact Sheets* (accessed 14 September 2021).

Figure 4: Example of a Change in the Star Rating Score with No Change in the Star Rating

15.67 → 13.06

17% reduction in risk of fatalities and serious injuries

Note: 1-Star is highest risk and 5-Star is lowest risk.
Sources: International Road Assessment Programme (iRAP) and Safe System Solutions Pty Ltd.

(ii) **Raw and smoothed Star Ratings.** In the iRAP methodology, an SRS and a Star Rating are calculated for each 100-meter (m) segment of road for vehicles occupants, motorcyclists, pedestrians, and bicyclists. These SRS and Star Ratings that apply to individual 100 m segments are known as *raw*. However, for the purposes of producing large maps and setting road safety performance targets, raw SRS and Star Ratings are averaged over longer lengths to produce *smoothed* results. This smoothing may be produced for predefined road segments (such as those defined in a road authority asset system) or by homogeneous lengths. The effect of smoothing is illustrated in Figure 5. This figure shows raw SRS in gray and smoothed SRS in white, along with the colored Star Rating bands. The "spikes" in the raw SRS are smoothed out in this process, noting that these spikes are associated generally with intersections.

(iii) **Star Ratings when there is zero flow.** Star Ratings are only produced where there is a flow recorded for the corresponding road user type. For example, if pedestrians do not walk or cross a section of road, then a Star Rating will not be produced for that length (i.e., the SRS will be zero). Along a road or design, it is therefore possible to have sections with a Star Rating interspersed with sections that have no Star Rating for a particular road user type. When reporting the Star Rating as a percentage of the design length it is suggested that the percentage is based on the length where the road user is present, and not the whole length of the design. For example, if a design is 10 km in length but pedestrians are expected to be present on only 5 km of that length, and if the 5 km length half is rated 3-Star, then it can be said that 50% of the design length is rated 3-Star for pedestrians (2.5 km/5 km).

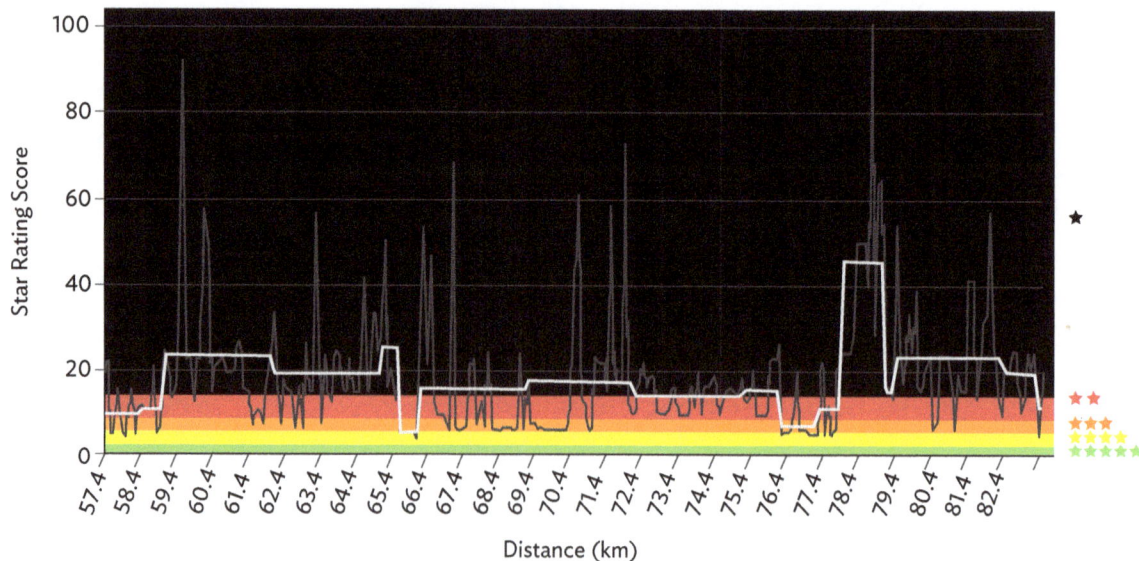

Figure 5: Raw and Smoothed Star Rating Scores

km = kilometer, SRS = Star rating score.
Note: 1-Star is highest risk and 5-Star is lowest risk. The gray curve corresponds to raw SRS while the white curve corresponds to smoothed SRS.
Source: International Road Assessment Programme (iRAP). 2021. *iRAP Methodology Fact Sheets* (accessed 14 September 2021).

A. Level 1 SR4RSA: Production of Star Ratings Associated with Each of the Specific Safety Concerns and Recommendations Identified in the Road Safety Audit

RSAs involve preparation of a table listing safety concerns and recommendations. The Level 1 SR4RSA approach involves adding Star Ratings and SRS for each safety concern and recommendation to the table. These are added for both the existing design (i.e., the design without any recommendations being implemented) and for the design with recommendations implemented. The Star Ratings and SRS are produced using the *Star Rating Demonstrator* (Box 2). The Level 1 process is illustrated in Figure 6 and an example of a SR4RSA safety concerns and recommendations table incorporating Star Ratings and SRS is shown in Figure 7.

As discussed in the *CAREC RSE Manual 1*, the safety concerns and recommendations table includes a "risk" column. This risk score for each safety concern is produced by the audit team to assist with prioritizing safety concerns, and is dependent on the professional

judgment of the audit team. Although there may be some overlap between this "risk" score and the Star Ratings and SRS, it is recommended that the risk column still be produced, for two reasons:

(i)   There are times when a Star Rating cannot be produced for a recommendation (see Chapter 10).
(ii)   The professional judgment of the audit team is valuable, and it can result in more information than may be able to be captured in the Star Ratings.

The client is required to respond in writing to each safety concern and recommendation contained in the audit report's table. The client's response should then be documented in the "Client Response" column of the table. The addition of the Star Rating information for each safety concern and recommendation provides the client with valuable objective information that can better inform their response. Responses can generally be grouped into the following categories:

(i)   acceptance of the recommendation,
(ii)   acceptance of the safety concern but does not agree with the recommendation, and
(iii) nonacceptance of the safety concern and recommendation.

Box 2: What Is the Star Rating Demonstrator?

The Star Rating Demonstrator is a freely available tool with the International Road Assessment Programme (iRAP) online software, ViDA.[a] With the Star Rating Demonstrator, it is possible to produce Star Ratings and Star rating scores (SRS) for a 100-meter length of road or design (that is, it produces raw results). Attributes such as lane widths, sidewalks, intersection layouts, and speeds can be adjusted for immediate feedback on the impact on the Star Ratings and SRS for vehicle occupants, motorcyclists, pedestrians, and bicyclists. Detailed definitions for each of the road attributes (which are grouped into six categories: roadside, midblock, intersections, vulnerable road user facilities and land use, and speeds) are available in the iRAP Coding Manual.[b]

Box Figure 2.1: Star Rating Demonstrator

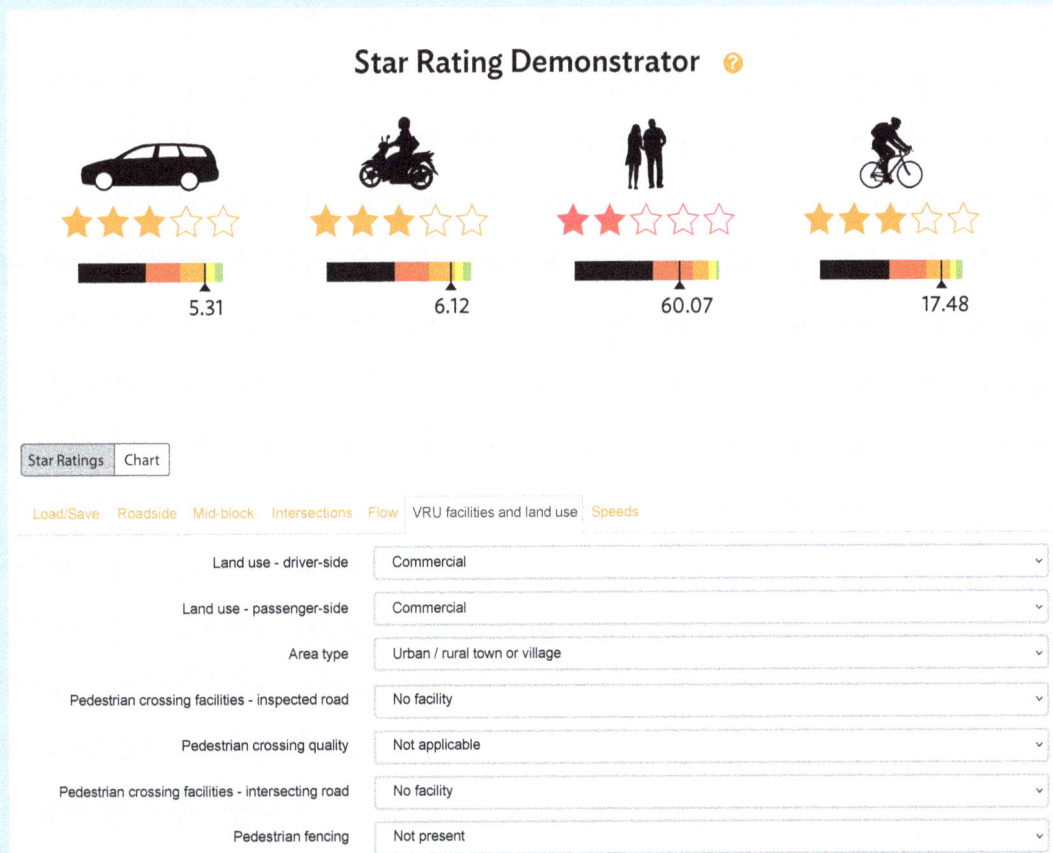

Note: 1-Star is highest risk and 5-Star is lowest risk.

Apart from presenting the Star Ratings for each road user, the Star Rating Demonstrator also presents SRS numerically and in chart form, illustrating the relative risk by crash type (e.g., head-on and run-off road risk for vehicle occupants, walking along the road, and crossing the road risk for pedestrians, etc.). This provides insight into how risk for specific types of crashes may be reduced by modifying road or design attributes.

[a] iRAP. 2021. iRAP Star Rating Demonstrator (accessed 14 September 2021).
[b] iRAP. 2021. iRAP Specification, Manuals and Guides (accessed 14 September 2021).

Source: International Road Assessment Programme (iRAP).

Figure 6: Level 1 Star Rating for Road Safety Audit Process

RSA = road safety audit.
Note: The Level 1 approach involves producing Star Ratings associated with each of the specific safety concerns and recommendations identified in the RSA. The Level 2 approach adds production of Star Ratings for the length of the design, with and without the RSA recommendations.
Sources: International Road Assessment Programme (iRAP) and Safe System Solutions Pty Ltd.

Figure 7: Example of Road Safety Audit Safety Concerns and Recommendations with Star Ratings and Star Rating Scores

Ref	Safety Concern	Risk	Star Rating (Initial Design)	Recommendation	Star Rating (With Recommendation)	Client Response
1.1	At Kilometer 15+710, a median opening and a T-intersection are proposed for access to the village access road. The median opening will also serve as a U-turn opportunity. However, there are no sheltered left-turn lanes proposed in the median for either direction. This may result in rear-end collisions at this location as vehicles slow down to turn from the "fast" lane. The risk of this crash is increased due to the speed of vehicles. 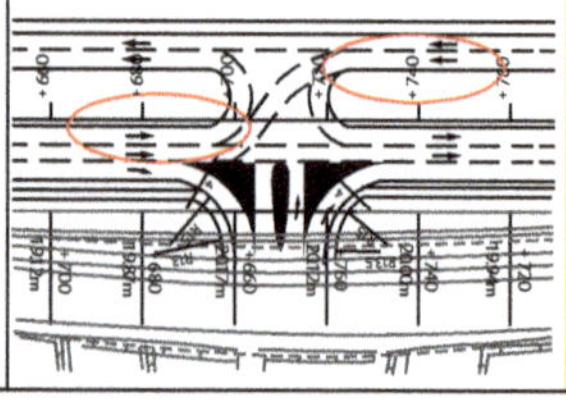	Medium	7.51 / 10.71 / 58.26 / 17.24	• Provide sheltered left-turn lanes on both approaches to the break in the median.	3.28 / 4.86 / 27.17 / 8.25	

Sources: International Road Assessment Programme (iRAP) and Safe System Solutions.

Benefits of the SR4RSA Level 1 approach include the following:

(i)   Star Ratings and SRS are produced for each road user type for each safety concern and recommendation. This provides the client, design team, and audit team with an evidence-based safety assessment and a measurement of the likely impact of recommendations.
(ii)   The audit team may be prompted to consider safety concerns and options that might not have been considered otherwise, particularly for vulnerable road users.
(iii) Star Ratings and SRS can be produced for a safety concern at a point location using the Star Rating Demonstrator in a matter of minutes.

In the SR4RSA Level 1 approach, the following should be considered:

(i)   Star Ratings and SRS are limited to the road safety attributes in the iRAP methodology. Other road safety concerns or findings will not be quantified using Star Ratings.
(ii)   Fatality and serious injury estimations and investment plans are not produced.
(iii) Because the Star Ratings and SRS are produced only for safety concerns and recommendations, and not for the entire length of the design, the approach cannot be used to measure the overall Star Rating of the design. It therefore cannot be used as a formal measure against a Star Rating target, but it does provide a partial indicator of how well the design is likely to perform against a target and relative impact of the recommendations.

1. Level 1 Worked Example (Road Design)

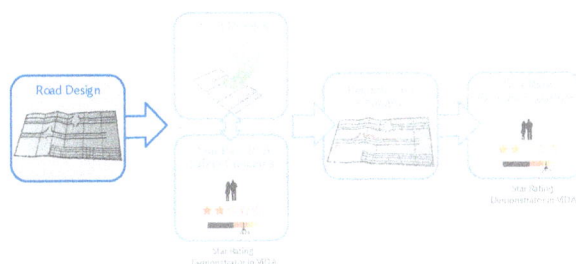

This worked example draws on iRAP assessment and design project data and was developed for the purpose of demonstrating the application of Level 1 SR4RSA concept. A road corridor is to be upgraded as part of an urban transport investment package. The proposed highway is a two-lane undivided cross section with a design speed of 100 kilometers per hour (kph). The preferred alignment is through undeveloped areas with a bridge spanning a river.

Key parameters of the design are as follows (Figure 8):

(i)   Design speed: 100 kph (speed limit to be 100 kph)
(ii)   Design stage received: Feasibility concepts and sketches
(iii) Lane width: 3.75 m
(iv)   Shoulders: 2.5 m
(v)   Central median: Center line
(vi)   Roadside: Roadside barriers (generally continuous) with some open roadsides and some roadside objects
(vii) Intersections: Grade-separated interchanges for major interchanges, unsignalized T-intersections for minor side roads with channelized turn lanes
(viii) Vulnerable road user facilities: Pedestrian and bicyclists traffic flow is low; however, there are paths linking townships to travel generating areas

2. Level 1 Worked Example (Audit Designs and Star Rate Road Safety Audit Safety Concerns)

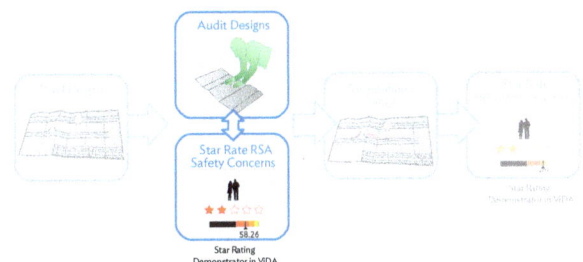

Consultants who were completely independent of the project were engaged to undertake a concept design stage Level 1 SR4RSA. They assembled an audit team consisting of individuals skilled, qualified, and knowledgeable in both RSA and the iRAP methodology. The team was composed of an audit team leader (a senior road safety auditor and iRAP-accredited) and audit team members (an international road safety auditor and a local road safety auditor).

A feasibility study report and associated designs were provided to the audit team who then reviewed the documents. While performing the audit, the team used the Star Rating Demonstrator in ViDA to quantify the seriousness of the road safety concerns identified.

Figure 8: Level 1 Worked Example of Typical Cross Section

SINGLE TWO-LANE CARRIAGEWAY
ESCALA 1:50

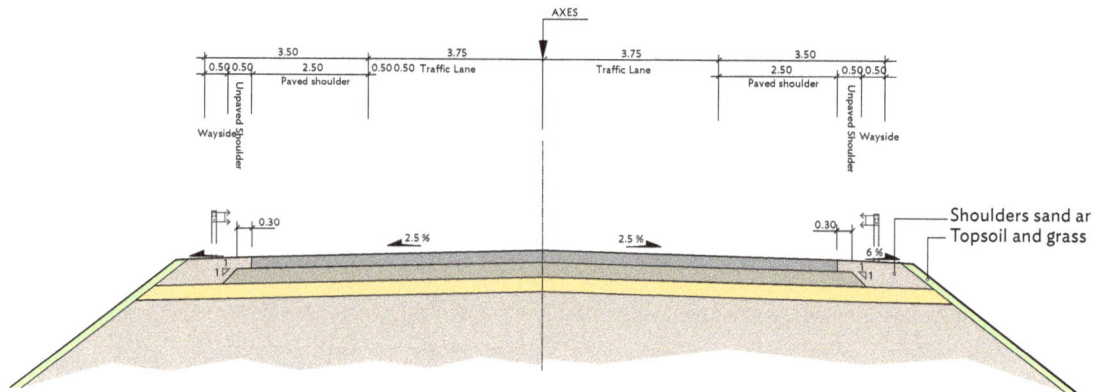

Source: International Road Assessment Programme (iRAP). 2017. *Sustainable Urban Transport Investment Program (SUTIP), Georgia: Road Safety Assessment of Preliminary Rioni Bridge Designs and Poti Town Roads.* London.

---

3. Level 1 Worked Example (Recommend and Star Rate Changes)

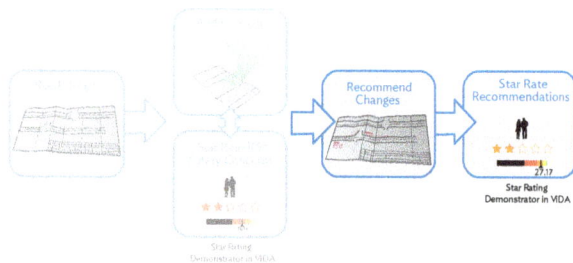

Following the identification and quantification of road safety concerns, the audit team then developed countermeasure recommendations. The team referred to the Road Safety Toolkit (https://toolkit.irap.org) to help identify effective and practical countermeasures, and used the Star Rating Demonstrator to quantify the impact of recommendations.

Figure 9 is an example of one set of safety concerns identified by the audit team and their recommended countermeasures. In this example, the safety concerns relate to the risk associated with vehicles running off the side of the road. Specifically, they relate to the designs for posts and associated footings, road safety barrier-end terminals, ditches, and embankments.

The audit team discussed the issues and determined that the risk rating for this safety concern was "high" by using the risk matrix contained in the *CAREC RSE Manual 1*.

To determine the initial design Star Ratings (i.e., without recommended interventions), the audit team used the Star Rating Demonstrator to define the typical cross section of the road design and vehicle operating speed. It is noted that in this example, the audit team assumed that the vehicle operating speed is the same as the design speed limit of 100 kph (see section 10.5). The results from the Star Rating Demonstrator indicated that the road cross section achieves a 2-Star rating for vehicle occupants and a 1-Star rating each for motorcyclists, pedestrians, and cyclists.

The qualitative recommendations made by the audit team are as follows:

(i)   ensure that objects located adjacent and near the road are frangible (i.e., breakable) or that the object is a roadside barrier;
(ii)   ensure roadside slopes are not steep;
(iii) apply shoulder audio-tactile line-markings (also known as raised-profile edge-lines);
(iv)   install energy-absorbing safety barrier-end treatments; and
(v)   install curve or chevron alignment markers.

Figure 9: Level 1 Worked Example of Roadside Safety Concerns and Recommendations Table

Ref	Safety Concern	Risk	Star Rating (Initial Design)	Recommendation	Star Rating (With Recommendation)	Client Response
1.7	There are a number of structures and roadside objects included in the drawings that will constitute roadside hazards, such as poles, turned-down safety barrier ends, culverts, and drains. Snips from the drawings of typical designs in the feasibility study are reproduced below. It is noted that the poles in the images below may be a "slip base" design, which is lower risk, but it is not clear from the designs and documentation. Standard design posts and post base 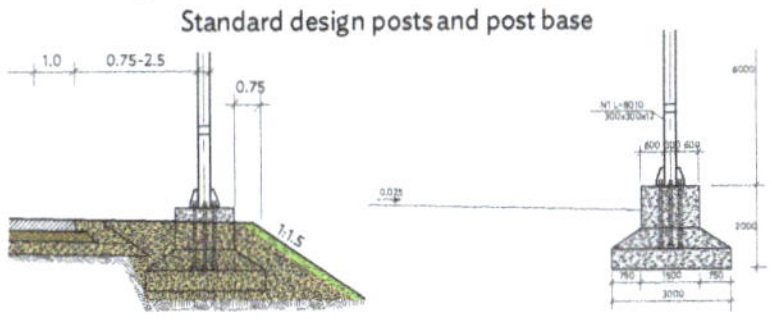 Standard design for barrier ramped end terminal 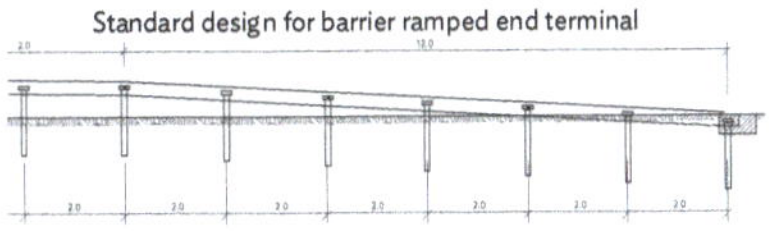 Standard design for ditch and embankment 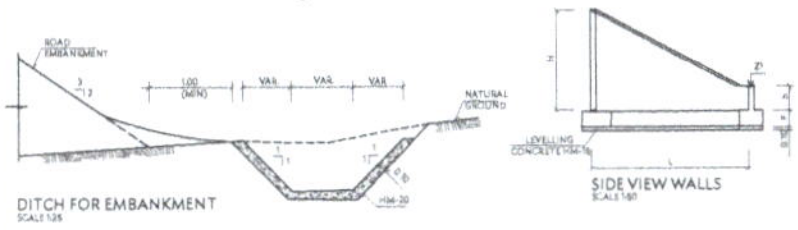	High	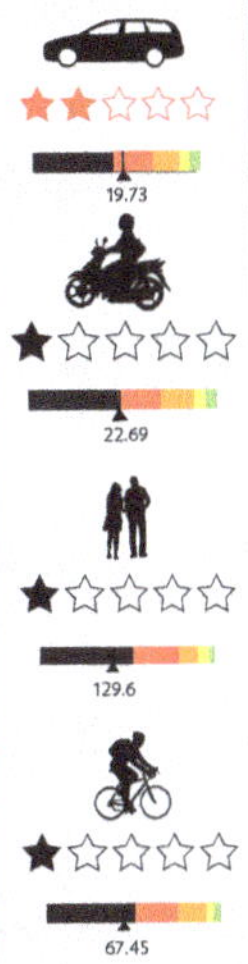 (car) ★★☆☆☆ 19.73 (motorcycle) ★☆☆☆☆ 22.69 (pedestrians) ★☆☆☆☆ 129.6 (bicycle) ★☆☆☆☆ 67.45	In order to reduce run road risks, consideration should be given to the following: • Using only frangible objects in the roadsides. Where nonfrangible objects must be used, safety barriers should be used. • Ensuring that roadside slopes are less than 1:4. Where steeper slopes are necessary, safety barriers should be used. • Using shoulder rumble strips, also known as raised profile edge markings or audio edge lines to delineate the road edge. • Using energy-absorbing safety barrier end treatments rather than turned down ends. • Installation of curve alignment marker signs on curves.	 (car) ★★★☆☆ 6.25 (motorcycle) ★★★☆☆ 12.15 (pedestrians) ★☆☆☆☆ 109.93 (bicycle) ★★☆☆☆ 44.96	

Note: 1-Star is highest risk and 5-Star is lowest risk.
Sources: International Road Assessment Programme (iRAP) and Safe System Solutions Pty Ltd.

Roadside signs on a highway in hilly area in Pakistan (photo by Zaheer Uddin).

Using the Star Rating Demonstrator, the audit team made the following specific recommendations:

(i)   The SRS for vehicle occupants reduced from 19.73 (2-Star) to 6.25 (3-Star). This represents a 68% reduction in fatality and serious injury risk.
(ii) The SRS for motorcyclists reduced by 46%, and the Star Rating increased from 1-Star to 3-Star.
(iii) The SRS for bicyclists reduced by 33% and the Star Rating for improved from 1-Star to 2-Star.
(iv) The pedestrian SRS reduced by 15%, however, the rating remained at 1-Star.

The installation of a road safety barrier had improved pedestrian safety by reducing the likelihood of vehicles running off the side of the road and striking a pedestrian. However, the Star Rating for pedestrians remained at 1-star. As such, the audit team produced separate and pedestrian-specific list of recommendations.

The audit team noted as the Star Ratings and SRS produced in the report are raw, they are therefore only indicative of the potential overall Star Ratings for the design.

B.   Level 2 SR4RSA: Production of Star Ratings for the Length of the Design, with and without the Road Safety Audit Recommendations

The Level 2 SR4RSA builds on the Level 1 SR4RSA by producing SRS and Star Ratings for the whole length of the road design rather than just for specific safety concerns and recommendations.

The Level 2 process is illustrated in Figure 10.

Level 2 SR4RSA assessments are primarily performed using the Star Rating for Design (SR4D) application within ViDA (see Box 3). This enables road attributes to be coded along the entire length of the design and allowing both the raw and *smoothed* SRS and Star Ratings to be produced. ViDA also produces interactive reports that can be used for enhanced analyses and communications.

In addition to the reports and maps that are produced in ViDA, the audit team may still consider producing an RSA table listing safety concerns and recommendations that includes the Star Ratings and SRS (as described for the Level 1 SR4RSA).

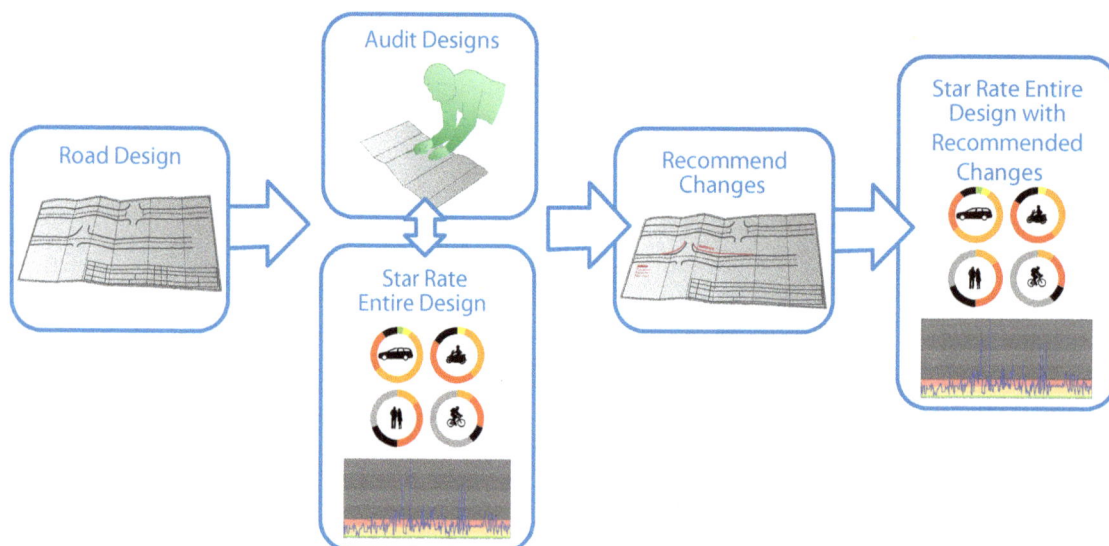

Figure 10: Level 2 Star Rating for Road Safety Audit Process

RSA = road safety audit.
Note: The Level 2 approach adds production of Star Ratings for the length of the design, with and without the RSA recommendations.
Sources: International Road Assessment Programme (iRAP) and Safe System Solutions Pty Ltd.

Benefits of the SR4RSA Level 2 approach include the following:

(i) Star Ratings and SRS are produced for each road user type for the entire design. This provides the client, design team, and audit team with relatable and evidence-based safety metrics for the design with and without recommendation scenarios.

(ii) The audit team is prompted to consider safety concerns that might otherwise have been overlooked, especially those involving vulnerable road users.

(iii) Both *raw* and *smoothed* Star Ratings are produced, meaning performance against safety targets is possible.

(iv) Interactive reports are produced for the whole design length.

(v) The Star Ratings assessment can often be performed relatively quickly.

In the SR4RSA Level 2 approach, the following should be considered:

(i) Fatality and serious injury estimations and investment plans are not the focus output, rather it is Star Ratings and SRS.

(ii) A higher level of training than the Level 1 approach is required and is ideally performed by someone who is iRAP-accredited.

The grand Karakoram Highway connects the People's Republic of China and Pakistan (photo by Ghulam Hussain).

Box 3: Star Rating for Design Web App

The Star Rating for Design (SR4D) application is a freely available tool within the International Road Assessment Programme (iRAP) online software, ViDA.[a] The tool was developed by iRAP with funding support from the Global Road Safety Facility.

The SR4D can be applied by any suitably trained engineer or road safety practitioner and is easily incorporated into the road design process. SR4D provides an objective Star Rating for each road user type (pedestrian, vehicle occupant, motorcyclist, and bicyclist) based on different road design elements that are drawn from proposed designs and coded by users. Key design elements are selected with a "click" from a menu of options.

For example, Box Figure 3.1 shows various options for roadside safety including roadside objects, offset distances to objects, and paved shoulder conditions. After the design attributes are recorded, the tool uses the iRAP methodology to generate the Star rating score or Star Rating, an approach that provides repeatable qualification of road user risk. In addition to the Star Ratings, the method can also be used to produce statistics on various safety-related road attributes (such as percentage of road or road design with good quality pedestrian crossings); estimates of the numbers of fatalities and serious injuries associated with the designs, including identification of locations where numbers a likely to be highest and lowest; and safer roads investment plans that list safety countermeasures that could be viably added to the design to improve safety within a specified budget. Star Ratings can be used to set an objective "pass mark" for designs.

Box Figure 3.1: Illustration of Various Road Safety Options

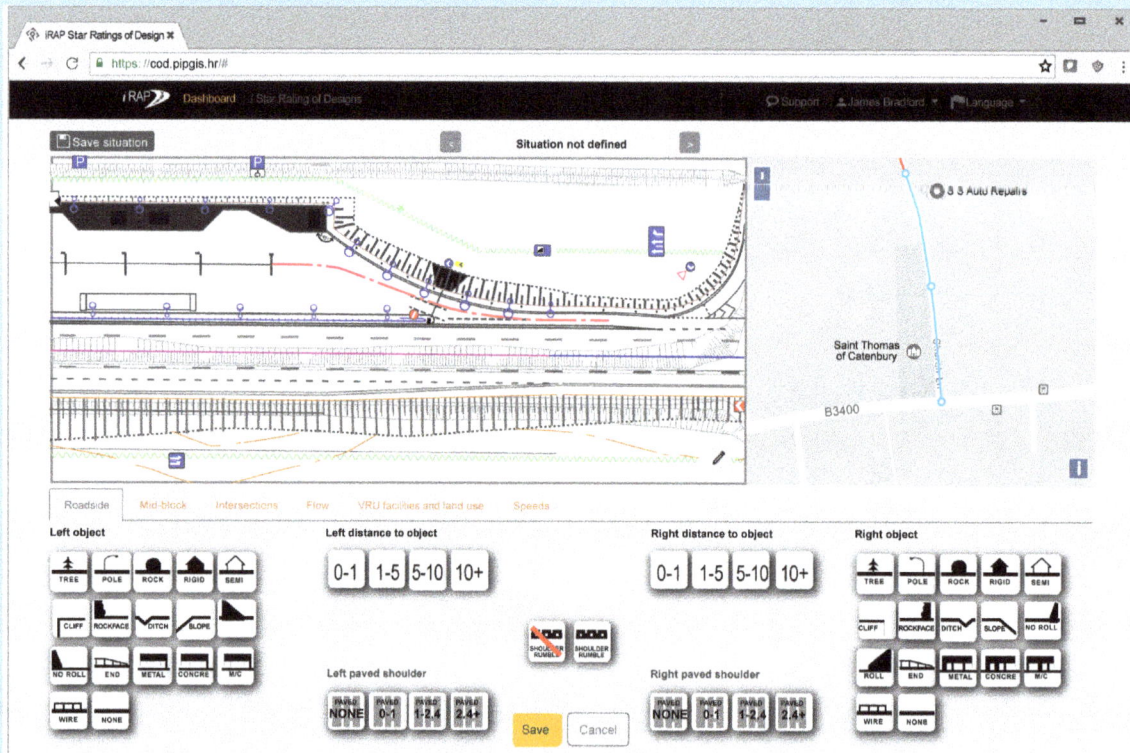

[a] iRAP. 2021. Welcome to ViDA. The iRAP Online Software to Help Create a World Free of High-Risk Roads (accessed 14 September 2021).
Source: International Road Assessment Programme (iRAP).

1. Level 2 Worked Example (Road Design)

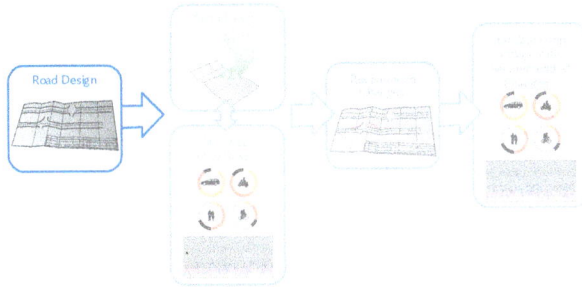

This worked example draws on iRAP assessment and design project data and was developed to demonstrate the application of Level 2 SR4RSA. A road corridor of 600 km between two major cities is to be upgraded from a two-lane undivided cross section to a four-lane dual carriageway cross section. The road corridor is predominantly rural and passes through a few towns. The upgraded road is to be constructed along the existing road alignment but deviated from it to accommodate topographical constraints and, in some instances, to bypass towns. The client had set the design team a target 3-Star or better rating for all road users for the design.

The key parameters of the design include the following (Figure 11):

(i)   Safety target: 3-Star or better
(ii)   Design speed: 110 kph
(iii)   Speed limit: 100 kph
(iv)   Design stage received: Preliminary design
(v)   Lane widths: 3.75 m
(vi)   Shoulders: 3.75 m passenger-side (0.75 m of which is being paved); 1.0 m paved driver-side
(vii) Central median: 3.0 m with semirigid, steel (w-beam type) safety barrier
(viii) Roadside: Embankments are 3.0 m maximum height with a 1:4 slope. Where proposed slope is steeper than 1:4 and at locations of culverts and rigid structures roadside safety barriers are included
(ix)   Intersections: Generally, incorporate merge and diverge lanes, include acceleration and deceleration lanes at the median crossing U-turn features. There are several channelized priority junctions that do not incorporate acceleration and/or deceleration lanes.
(x)   Vulnerable road user facilities: Limited facilities provided. Footpaths and crossings (both at-grade and grade-separated) are proposed at some of the bus stop locations in the towns.

Figure 11: Level 2 Worked Example of Typical Cross Section 2

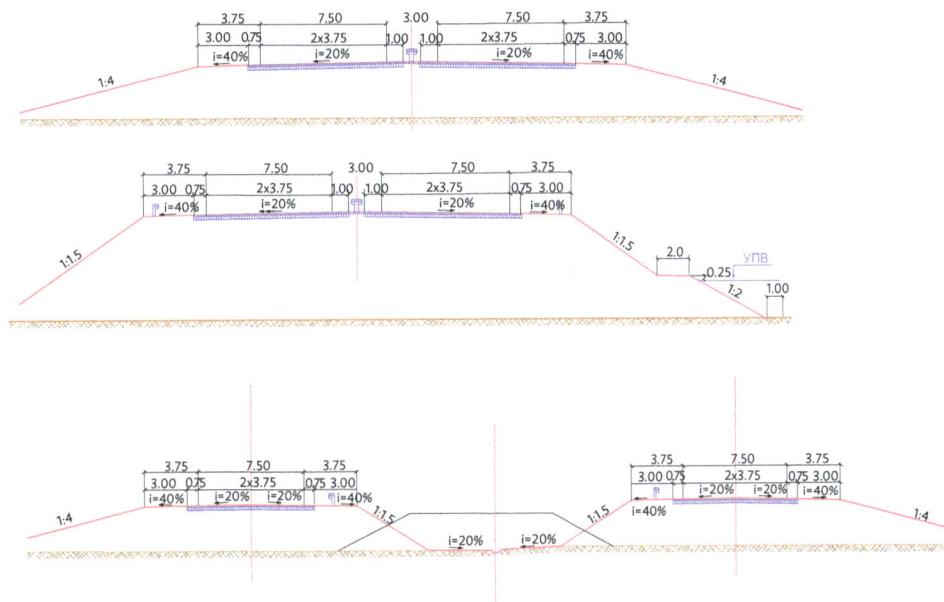

Source: International Road Assessment Programme (iRAP). 2017. *Center-South Corridor Kazakhstan: iRAP Design Star Rating Assessment.*

2. Level 2 Worked Example (Audit Designs and Star Rate Entire Design)

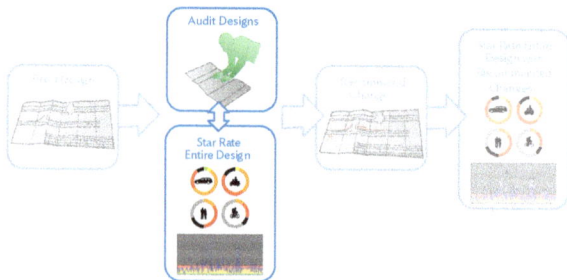

Road safety consultants were engaged by the client to perform a preliminary stage Level 2 SR4RSA, identify safety concerns, and provide recommendations to achieve a design of 3-Star or better. The consultant team is independent of the project and consists of members who are skilled, qualified, and knowledgeable in both RSAs and the iRAP methodology. The team was composed of an audit team leader (a senior road safety auditor and iRAP-accredited) and audit team members (an international road safety auditor and a local road safety auditor).

The designs were provided to the audit team who were briefed on the road environment by the client and design team. The audit team then performed a Star Rating of the design using the SR4D application in ViDA. The Star Ratings for the design results are summarized in Figure 12.

The Star Ratings allowed the audit team to identify the level of safety in the proposed design and identify road users who were at most risk. As can be seen in Figure 12, the design achieved a 3-Star or better rating for vehicle occupants. However, the design only achieved a 1-Star rating for motorcyclists and 2-Star for pedestrians. It is noted in this example that the pedestrian Star Rating was produced only for the sections of road that pedestrians would use. Further, no bicyclist Star Rating was produced as bicyclists would not be using the road.

Apart from the Star Ratings table, "risk worms" were also produced for the designs, as shown in Figure 13. This "risk worm" graph indicates how SRS and Star Ratings vary along each 100 m segment of the road design, allowing segments of road with low and high risk to be easily identified.

The audit team was able to utilize the output from assessment with the iRAP methodology to help identify specific safety concerns. Further, they performed both daytime and nighttime site inspections, focusing on locations with elevated risk. During this process, the audit team gained insights that enabled them to confirm assumptions that were made when performing the assessment using the iRAP methodology. For example, they confirmed that bicyclists would not be using the road. This iterative process, or situational scrutiny, is discussed further in Chapter 10.

Figure 12: Level 2 Worked Example of Smoothed Star Ratings for Existing Design

Filter 1 - iRAP > iRAP Kazakhstan > Center-South v3.02 > Center-South > 4 ···   Star Ratings

Star Ratings	Vehicle Occupant		Motorcyclist		Pedestrian		Bicyclist	
	Length (km)	Percent	Length (km)	Percent	Length (km)	Percent	Length (km)	Percent
5 Stars	0.00	0.00%	0.00	0.00%	0.00	0.00%	0.00	0.00%
4 Stars	1174.10	89.01%	0.00	0.00%	0.80	0.06%	0.00	0.00%
3 Stars	145.00	10.99%	0.00	0.00%	0.30	0.02%	0.00	0.00%
2 Stars	0.00	0.00%	1319.10	100.00%	0.00	0.00%	0.00	0.00%
1 Star	0.00	0.00%	0.00	0.00%	6.40	0.49%	0.00	0.00%
Not Applicable	0.00	0.00%	0.00	0.00%	1311.60	99.43%	1319.10	100.00%
Totals	1319.10	100.00%	1319.10	100.00%	1319.10	100.00%	1319.10	100.00%

(Bicyclist column: None present)

Note: 1-Star is highest risk and 5-Star is lowest risk.
Source: International Road Assessment Programme (iRAP).

Figure 13: Level 2 Worked Example of Raw Star Rating Scores and Star Ratings for the Existing Design

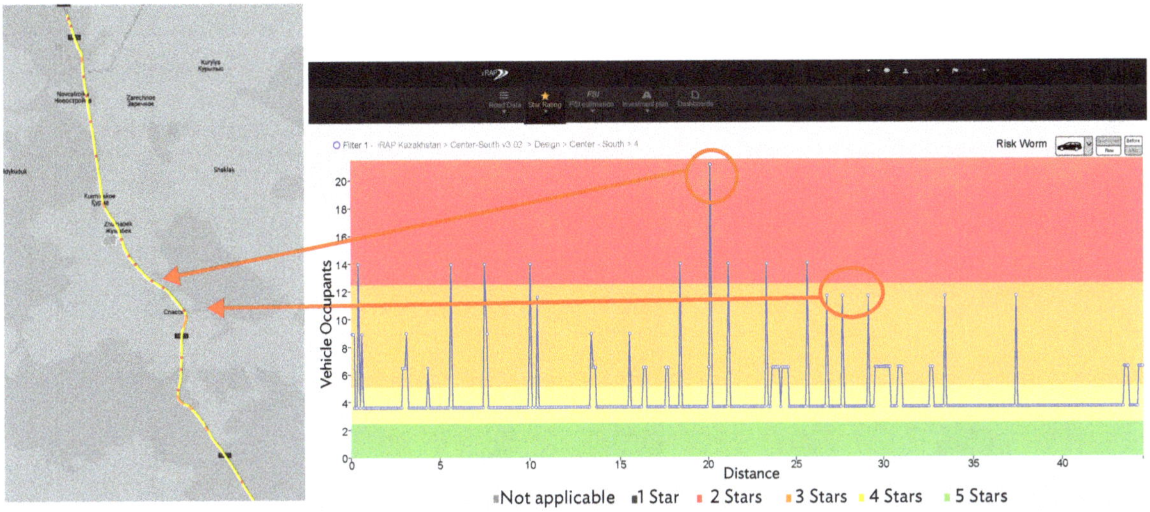

Sources: International Road Assessment Programme (iRAP) and Safe System Solutions Pty Ltd.

3. Level 2 Worked Example (Recommend Changes)

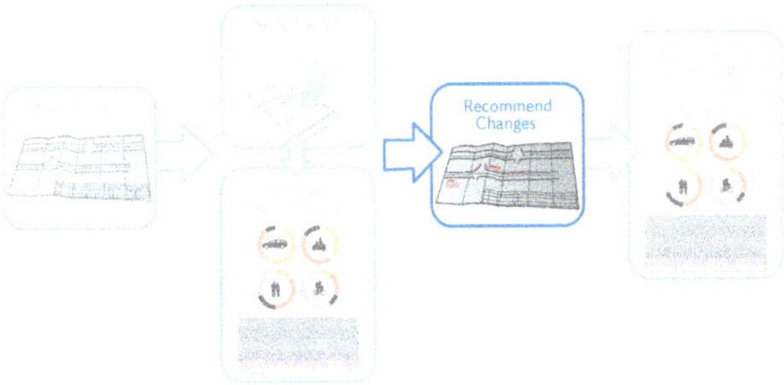

The audit team then developed recommendations for each safety concern. Their process of developing recommendations made use of the Road Safety Toolkit, which assisted the team to identify countermeasures that would be effective and practical.[24] The audit team also used the Star Rating Demonstrator to quantify the impact of their recommendations.

A report was then produced by the audit team following the guidelines in the CAREC RSE Manual 1 and including the results produced using the iRAP methodology.

Figure 14 and Figure 15 are examples of safety concerns and recommendations made by the audit team as well as the associated Star Ratings and SRS. The audit team noted that the raw Star Ratings for the recommendations in these tables relate to specific safety concerns and specific locations along the design. Therefore, they are only indicative of the overall smoothed Star Ratings for the design.

4. Level 2 Worked Example (Star Rate Entire Design with Recommended Changes)

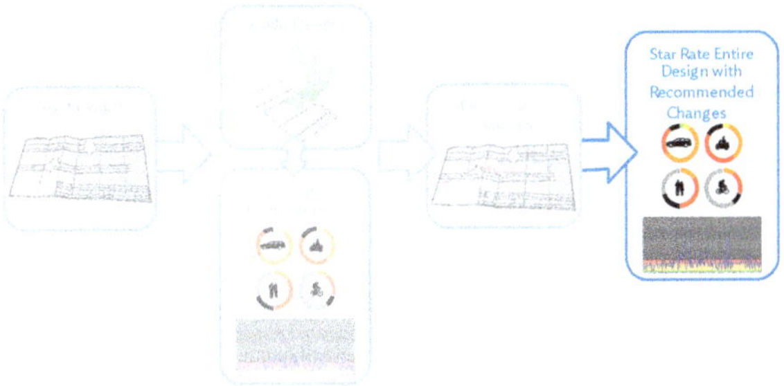

Once all the safety issues were documented and recommendations established, the SR4D software in ViDA was used to produce Star Ratings and

---

24   iRAP. 2021. Road Safety Toolkit (accessed 14 September 2021).

Figure 14: Level 2 Worked Example of Intersection Safety Concerns and Recommendations

Ref	Safety Concern	Risk	Star Rating (Initial Design)	Recommendation	Star Rating (With Recommendation)	Client Response
4.2	At Kilometer 38+93 it is proposed that a side road will join the main line. The west road connection includes acceleration and deceleration lanes; however, the road entering from the east (top of the design snip below) does not have acceleration lanes. Further, the exit and entry radii are very relaxed, increasing the entry speeds of vehicles entering from the side road. This may result in failure to give way crashes and rear end crashes. It will also encourage high movements onto the side road. This problem is exacerbated by the size of the junction and the lack of any physical islands within the junction; only road markings are proposed. This will increase the risk of "give way" conflicts. It will also increase the risk of vehicles entering the side road at high speed and losing control. This intersection contributed to an elevated Star rating score in this 100-m segment in the iRAP assessment for passenger vehicles and motorcyclists. 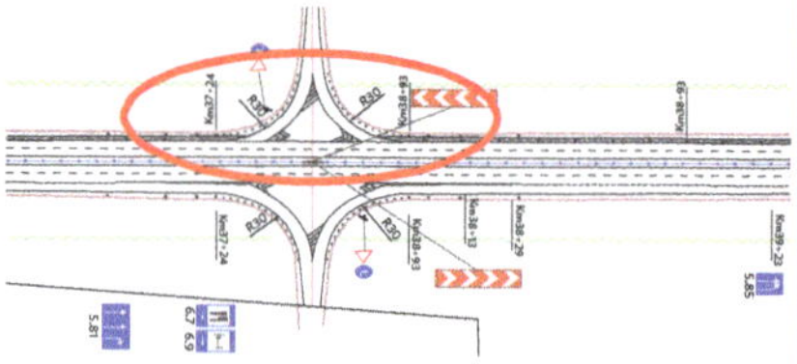	High	 ★☆☆☆☆ 74.22 / ★☆☆☆☆ 101.73 / ☆☆☆☆☆ NA / ☆☆☆☆☆ NA	• Provide sheltered acceleration and deceleration lanes for the east road. • Provide a physical (not painted) island within the junction to deter vehicle from crossing into opposing lanes.	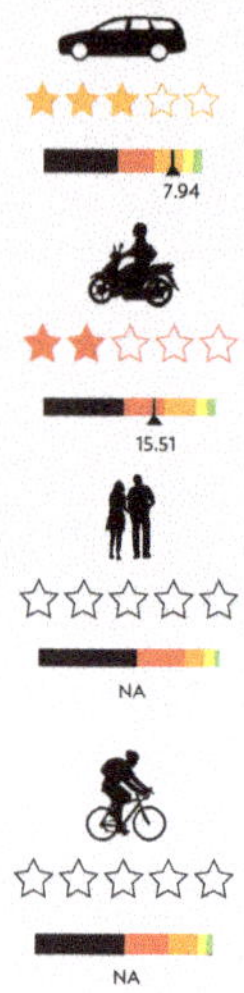 ★★★☆☆ 7.94 / ★★☆☆☆ 15.51 / ☆☆☆☆☆ NA / ☆☆☆☆☆ NA	

Sources: International Road Assessment Programme (iRAP) and Safe System Solutions Pty Ltd.

Figure 15: Level 2 Worked Example of Pedestrian Safety Concerns and Recommendations

Ref	Safety Concern	Risk	Star Rating (Initial Design)	Recommendation	Star Rating (With Recommendation)	Client Response
13.4	At Kilometer 40+400, 80+10, 170+5 and 330+650 pedestrian crossings have been proposed to link communities with bus stops. In most locations, these crossings straddle four lanes of high-speed traffic. The presence of the second lane will encourage overtaking in the vicinity of the crossings and potentially even higher speeds. There is also the possibility of dynamic visual obstruction (masking) where a pedestrian will not be seen due to another moving vehicle blocking sight lines. These combined factors will increase the risk of conflict between pedestrians and vehicles. At each of these locations, the speeds and number of lanes contributed to elevated Star rating score in the iRAP assessment for pedestrians. 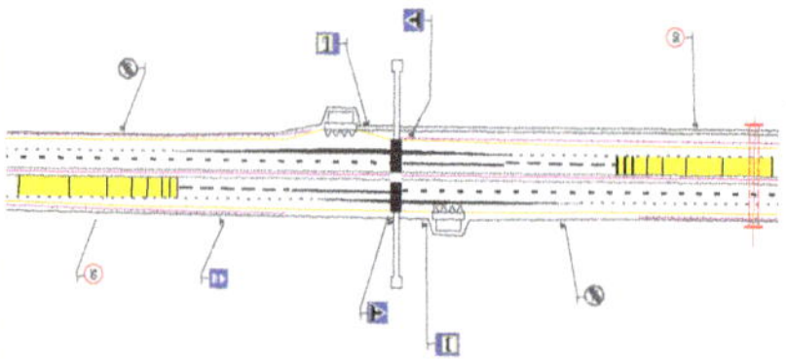	Very High	 ★★★★★ 1.51 / ★★★★☆ 4.54 / ★★☆☆☆ 60.26 / ☆☆☆☆☆ NA	• Reduce the carriageway from four to two lanes at these locations.	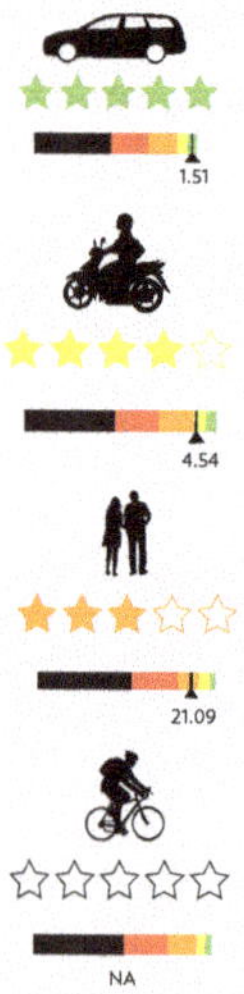 ★★★★★ 1.51 / ★★★★☆ 4.54 / ★★★☆☆ 21.09 / ☆☆☆☆☆ NA	

Sources: International Road Assessment Programme (iRAP) and Safe System Solutions Pty Ltd.

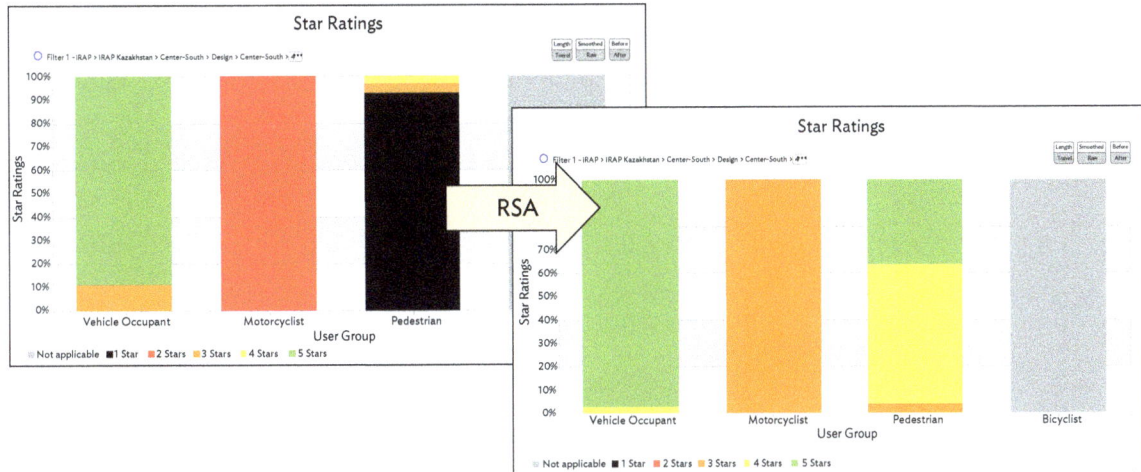

Figure 16: Level 2 Worked Example of Smoothed Star Ratings for the Existing Design and for Design with Recommendations

Note: 1-Star is highest risk and 5-Star is lowest risk.
Sources: International Road Assessment Programme (iRAP) and Safe System Solutions Pty Ltd.

recommendations for the entire length of the design. The results enabled the team to quantify the benefits of incorporating their recommendations into the design. The smoothed Star Ratings are shown in Figure 16.

Comparing the design with recommendations included to the existing design, the Star Ratings results indicate the following:

(i)   vehicle occupants would improve from 3-Star and 4-Star to 4-Star and 5-Star;
(ii)   motorcyclists would improve from 2-Star to 3-Star;
(iii) pedestrians would improve from 1-Star to 3-Star, and 4-Star to 5-Star (noting that the graph in Figure 16 only shows the percentage of road where pedestrians may be present).

There were no bicyclist Star Ratings produced as the audit team confirmed from their site inspection that bicyclists will not be using the road.

The result of this process is that the audit team reaffirmed that the design would achieve the target of 3-Star or better once all recommendations were incorporated.

C.   Level 3 SR4RSA: Production of Star Ratings, Fatality Estimations, and Investment Plans for the Length of the Design, with and without the Road Safety Audit Recommendations

The Level 3 SR4RSA builds on the Level 2 approach by adding an estimate of the change in fatal and serious injuries if the recommendations are included. The Level 3 approach also introduces the Safer Roads Investment Plan (SRIP), which assists with identifying safety countermeasure options and assessing economic costs and benefits. The Level 3 process is illustrated in Figure 17.

As with the Level 2 approach, the Level 3 approach involves an iRAP assessment of the entire length of the design and the analysis is performed with the SR4D application in ViDA.

Benefits of taking the Level 3 approach include the following:

(i)   Estimates of the numbers of fatalities and serious injuries along each 100 m segment of the design are produced for each road user type in addition to Star Ratings and Star rating scores. This provides the client, designer, and audit

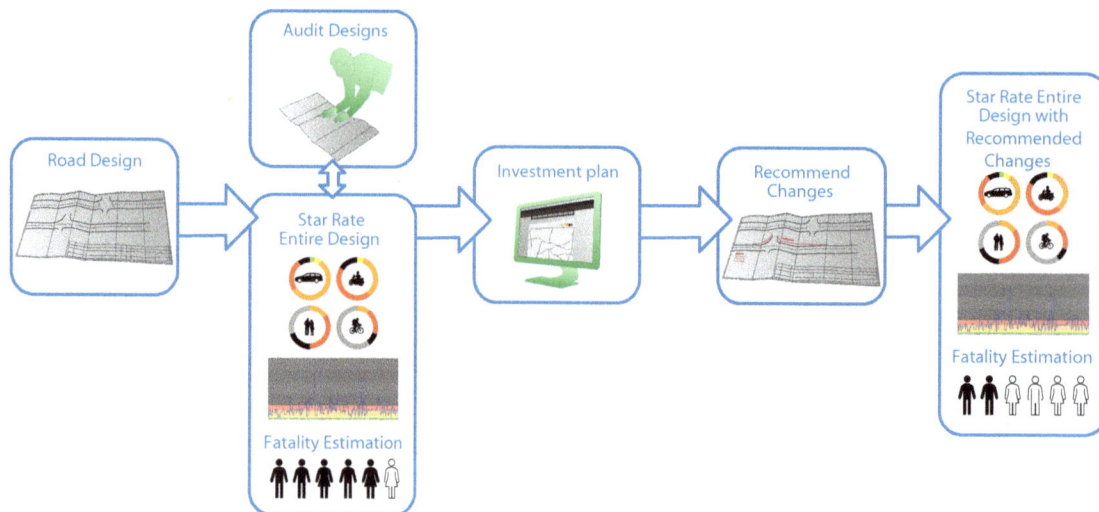

Figure 17: Level 3 Star Ratings for Road Safety Audit Process

Note: The Level 3 approach adds production of Star Ratings, fatality estimations, and investment plans for the length of the design, with and without the RSA recommendations. 1-Star is highest risk and 5-Star is lowest risk.
Sources: International Road Assessment Programme (iRAP) and Safe System Solutions Pty Ltd.

team with a relatable evidence-based measure of the likely safety performance of the design and impact of the recommendations.

(ii) SRIPs are produced providing the audit team with a list of countermeasure options and economic assessments for each 100 m segment of the design. The SRIP can be adjusted to match available budgets.

(iii) The audit team is often prompted to consider safety issues that might not have been considered otherwise, especially for vulnerable road users.

(iv) Can be used to measure if a safety performance target has been achieved.

In the SR4RSA Level 3 approach, the following should be considered:

(i) It requires more data and analysis than the Level 2 approach.

(ii) It requires a higher level of experience than the Level 2 approach and is ideally performed by someone who is iRAP-accredited.

1. Level 3 Worked Example (Road Design)

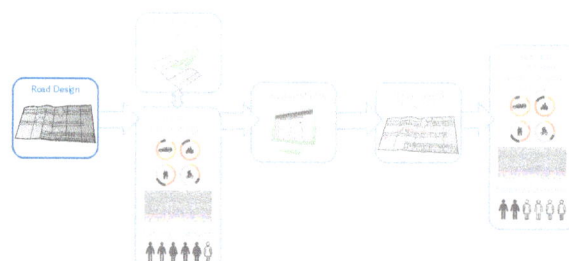

This worked example is an adaptation of information produced for the Central Highlands Connectivity Improvement Project, Viet Nam.[25] A 23 km section of a national highway that connects two major cities is to be upgraded to improve accessibility and road safety. The current highway is a two-lane undivided cross section. The upgraded highway will include a new "mixed lane" for bicyclists and motorcyclists on both sides, and opposing traffic flows are separated by a 150-millimeter centerline. In line with country's road safety strategy, the client had set the design team a target of a minimum 3-Star rating for all road users.

---

[25] The authors thank the World Bank Global Road Safety Facility and FRED Engineering for providing permission to use this project and adapt this information for this manual.

Following are the key aspects of the design (Figure 18):

(i)   Safety target: 3-Star or better
(ii) Design speeds: 40 km per hour (kph), 50 kph, and 70 kph
(iii) Design level received: detailed design
(iv) Lane widths: 3.5 m traffic lane, 2.5 m mixed lane
(v)   Shoulders: Narrow or none
(vi) Central median: None
(vii) Roadside: Embankments are 3.0 m maximum height with a 1:1.5 slope; road safety barriers are proposed over structures and at locations with high batters.
(viii) Vulnerable road user facilities: Footpaths and crossings, both at-grade and grade-separated, are proposed at some of the bus stops in towns and villages.

2. Level 3 Worked Example (Audit Designs and Star Rate Entire Design)

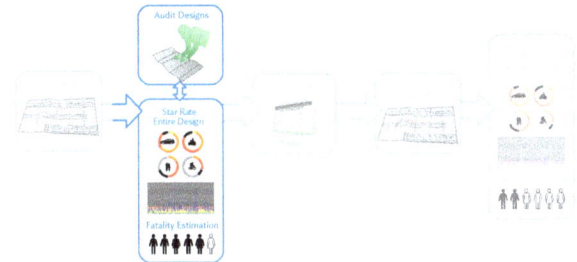

Consultants were engaged to perform a Level 3 SR4RSA to identify safety concerns and provide recommendations on the road design to achieve a 3-Star or better rating. The consultants are independent of the project and the design process. They assembled an audit team with individuals skilled, qualified, and knowledgeable in both RSA and the iRAP methodology. This team was composed of an audit team leader (a senior road safety auditor and iRAP-accredited) and audit team members (an international road safety auditor and a local road safety auditor).

Figure 18: Level 3 Worked Example of Typical Cross Section 3

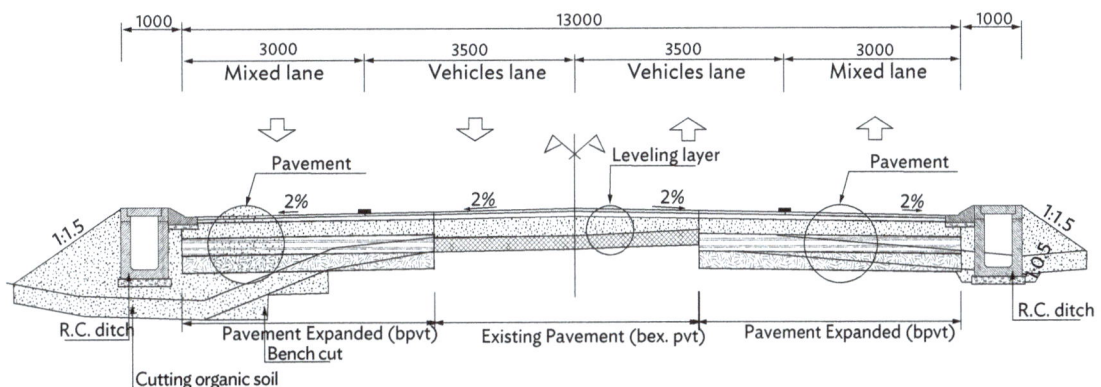

Source: FRED Engineering and Alta Planning and Design. 2020. Road Safety Assessment of NH19 Package CW3. Viet Nam.

The audit team were briefed on the road environment at an inception meeting with the client and design team. They were also provided with the designs, existing road traffic volumes, speed and fatal and serious injury data, typical countermeasure costs, and key economic data. The audit team then completed a desktop Star Rating of the design with SR4D in ViDA. The Star Ratings are presented in Figure 19. The black and red sections indicate areas where the design did not achieve the 3-Star target.

Figure 19: Level 3 Worked Example of Smoothed Star Ratings for Each Road User Type along the Existing Design

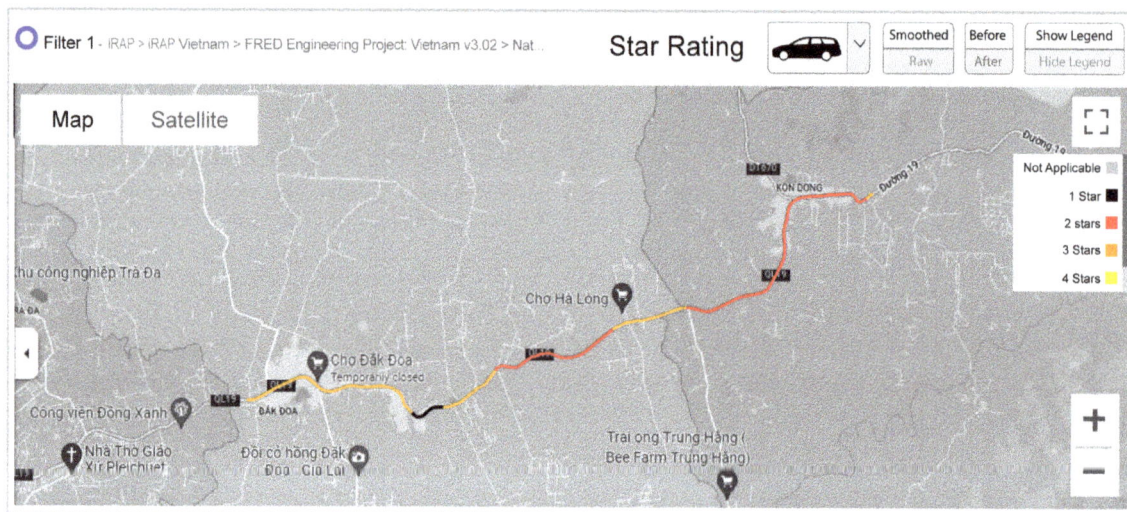

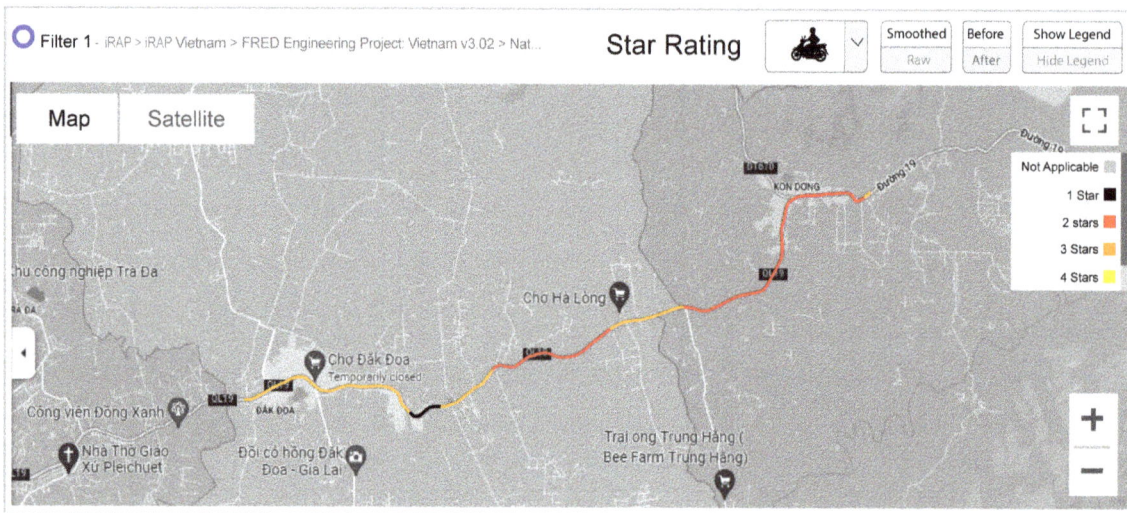

continued on next page

Figure 19: *continued*

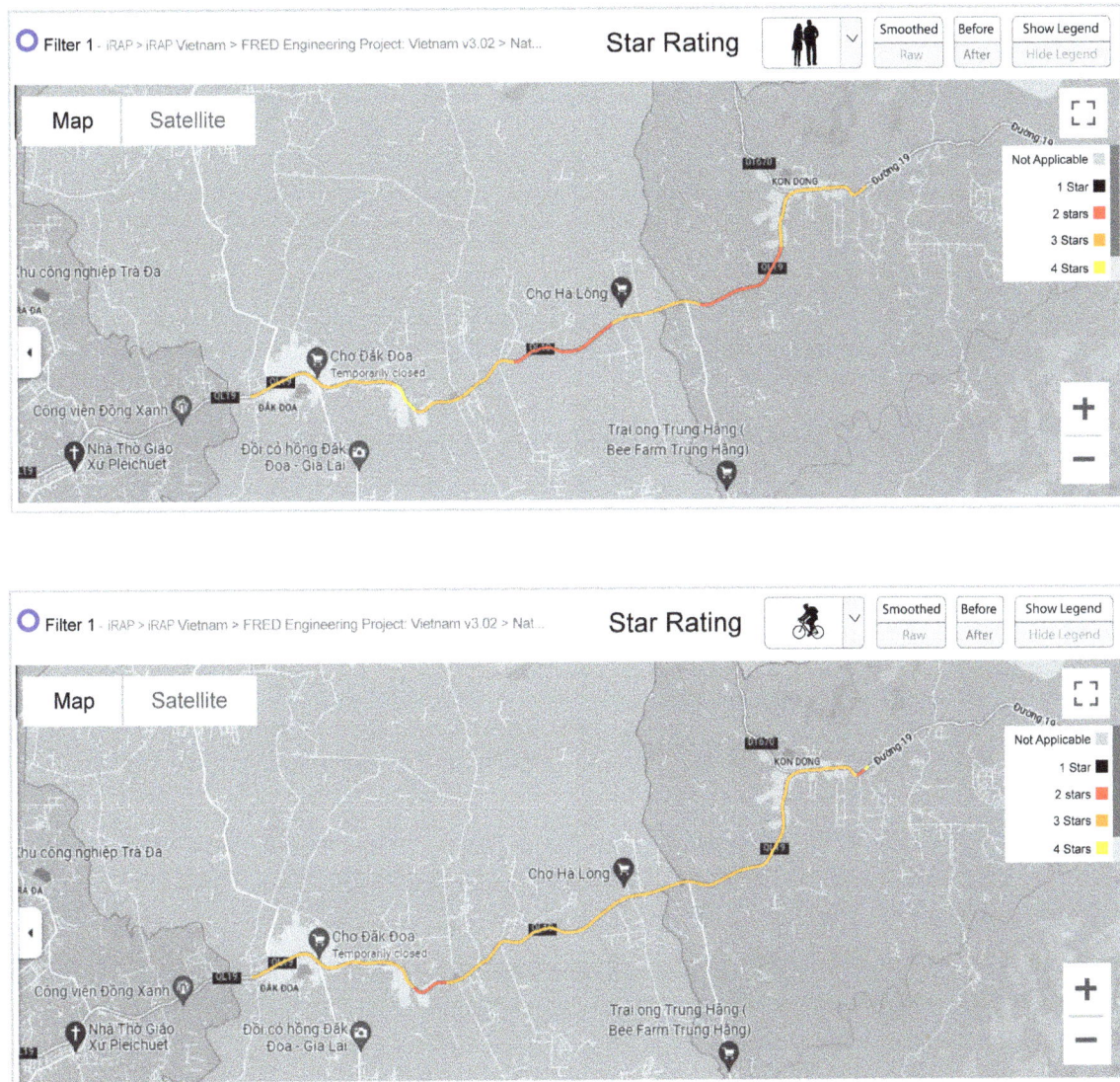

Note: 1-Star is highest risk and 5-Star is lowest risk.
Source: FRED Engineering and Alta Planning and Design (2020) in International Road Assessment Programme (iRAP). 2021. Welcome to ViDA. The iRAP Online Software to Help Create a World Free of High-Risk Roads (accessed 14 September 2021).

Raw SRS and corresponding raw Star Ratings for sections of the design were also produced, as illustrated in Figure 20. These data helped the audit team to identify segments of the design that have elevated risk and did not meet the target of 3-stars.

To gather further insights into the specifics of the risks at these points and the crash types of concern, the audit team used the Risk Worm by Crash Type function in ViDA to build a picture of crash risk, by crash type. Figure 21 depicts the output of a Risk Worm by Crash Type.

Figure 20: Level 3 Worked Example of Raw Star Rating Scores and Star Ratings for Motorcyclists and Bicyclists along Sections of the Design

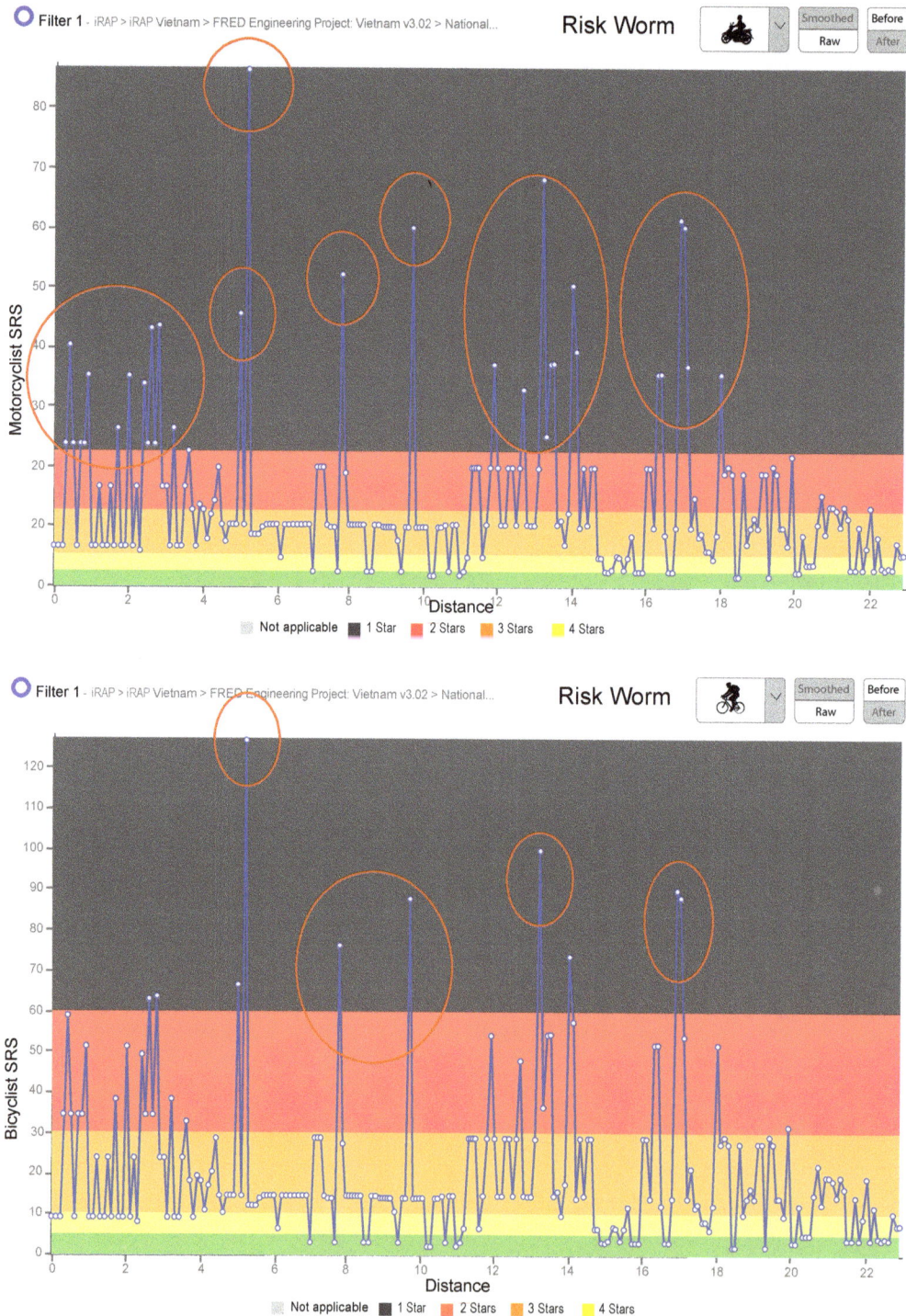

Notes: 1-Star is highest risk and 5-Star is lowest risk. The red circles identify segments with elevated risk.
Source: Adapted from FRED Engineering and Alta Planning and Design (2020) in International Road Assessment Programme (iRAP). 2021. Welcome to ViDA. The iRAP Online Software to Help Create a World Free of High-Risk Roads (accessed 14 September 2021).

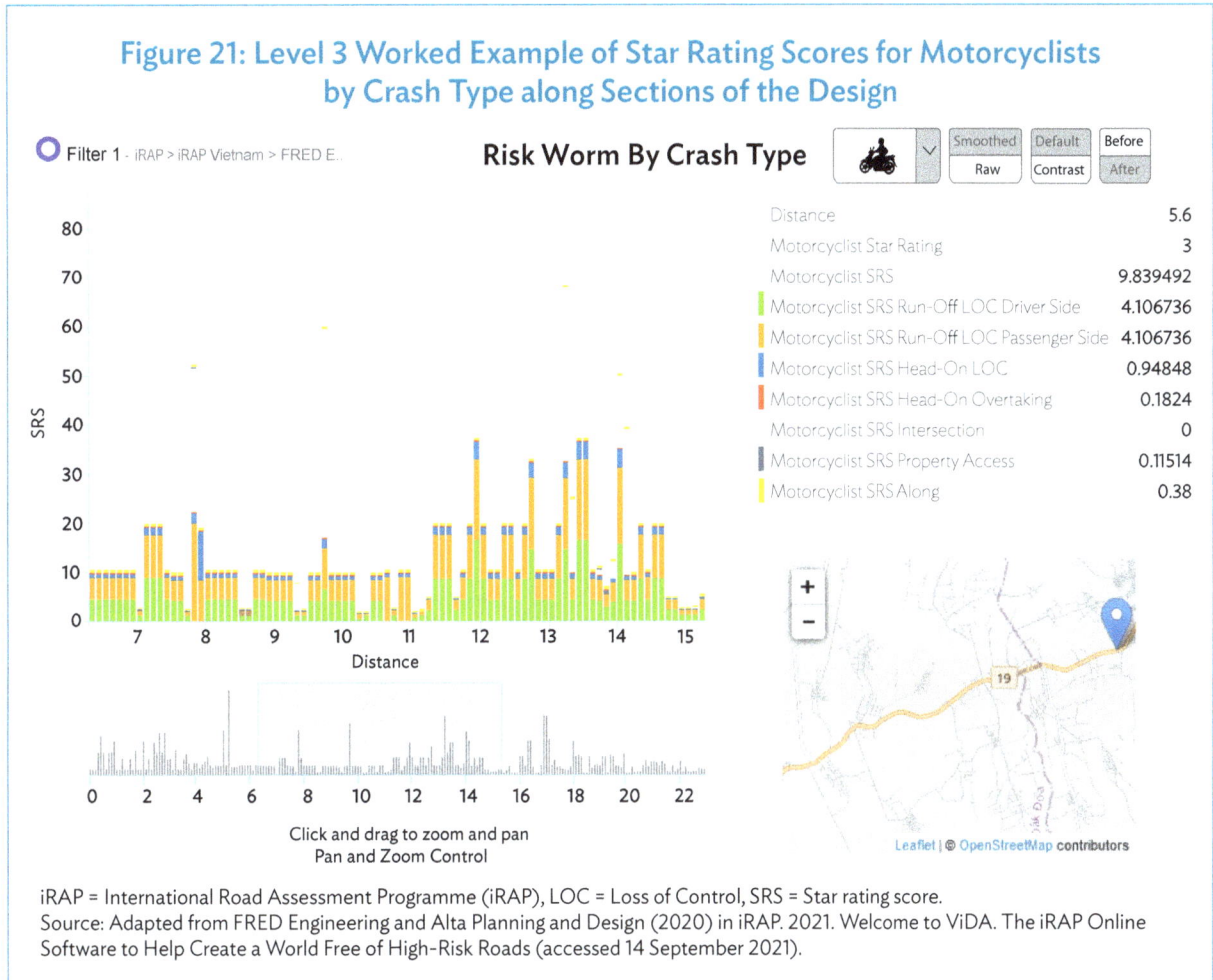

Figure 21: Level 3 Worked Example of Star Rating Scores for Motorcyclists by Crash Type along Sections of the Design

iRAP = International Road Assessment Programme (iRAP), LOC = Loss of Control, SRS = Star rating score.
Source: Adapted from FRED Engineering and Alta Planning and Design (2020) in iRAP. 2021. Welcome to ViDA. The iRAP Online Software to Help Create a World Free of High-Risk Roads (accessed 14 September 2021).

The audit team then used the iRAP methodology to estimate the numbers of fatalities and serious injuries along the design by combining SRS data, flow data, and network-level crash data. The results are illustrated in Figure 22. The segments with the highest number of fatalities and serious injuries are shown in purple and those with the lowest number are shown in light blue.

Data shown in Figure 26 helped the audit team by

(i)   highlighting sections of higher risk before a site visit is conducted and before detailed designs of the road had been produced;
(ii)   identifying road user class and associated crash types of the highest risk along the route; and
(iii)   providing a reference point for the target of achieving a minimum 3-Star rating for the entire route.

Using the iRAP Star Rating for Design information, the audit team followed the process set out in the *CAREC*

RSE Manual 1 to identify safety concerns, risk rate the concerns, and provide recommendations to address their concerns. They also produced Star Ratings for each set of safety concerns and their recommended countermeasures. These were documented in the RSA table. Three safety concerns were identified (Figure 23, Figure 24, and Figure 25):

(i)   **Rigid concrete guideposts that were included in the design.** These are a run-off-road hazard where posts with a diameter greater than 10 centimeters were recorded in the Star Rating Demonstrator as hazardous.

(ii)   **Transitions between safety barriers and bridge barriers lacked sufficient stiffening.** In the event it is struck by a vehicle, the safety barrier would deform excessively relative to the bridge barrier, thus creating a hazard. These were recorded in the Star Rating Demonstrator as unprotected safety barrier ends.

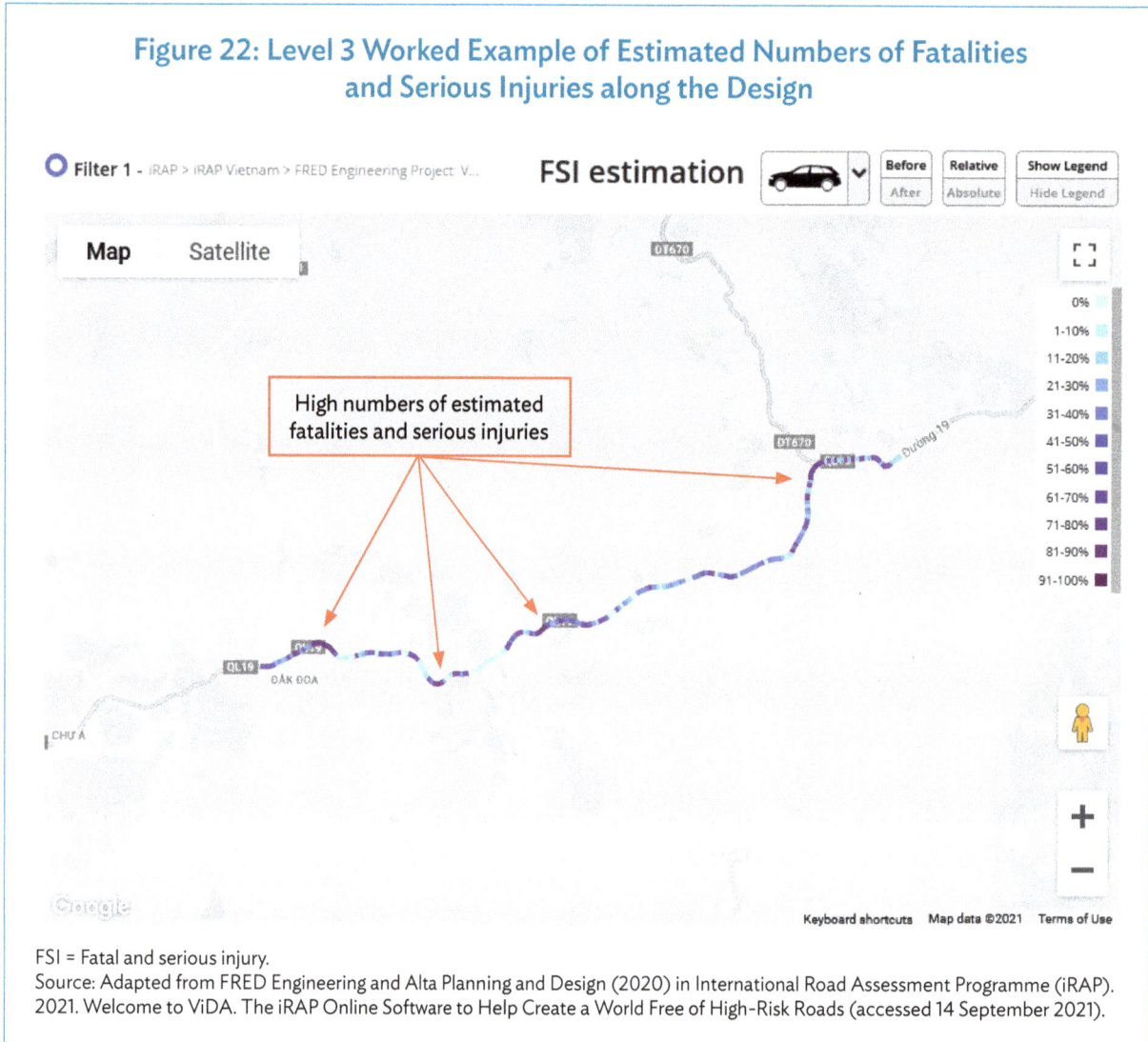

Figure 22: Level 3 Worked Example of Estimated Numbers of Fatalities and Serious Injuries along the Design

FSI = Fatal and serious injury.
Source: Adapted from FRED Engineering and Alta Planning and Design (2020) in International Road Assessment Programme (iRAP). 2021. Welcome to ViDA. The iRAP Online Software to Help Create a World Free of High-Risk Roads (accessed 14 September 2021).

(iii) **Proposed sidewalks were to be formed by placing covers on drainage channels.** These were judged by the audit team to be too narrow to accommodate the pedestrian flow. As such, this would result in pedestrians walking on the road rather than the sidewalk. This inadequate sidewalk was recorded in the Star Rating Demonstrator as being an informal sidewalk.

3. Level 3 Worked Example (Investment Plan)

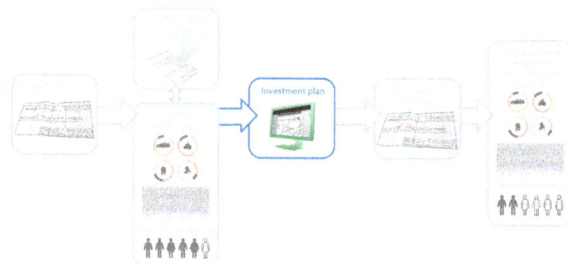

The audit team then used the iRAP methodology to create an SRIP for the design. This provided the audit team with a number of countermeasure options that could be introduced to the design to reduce risk and, in effect, achieve the 3-Star rating target. The audit team also acknowledged that the countermeasures needed to be affordable. As such, the audit team did set a budget for the SRIP that was consistent with available funding.

Examples of outputs from the SRIP are provided in Figure 23, Figure 24, and Figure 25. Figure 23 and Figure 24 indicate the locations at which traffic calming and roadside barriers (and/or safe end treatments) were to be considered. Figure 25 is an excerpt from the strip plan, which lists safety countermeasure options that were considered along each 100 m segment of the design.

Figure 23: Level 3 Worked Example of Locations Where Traffic-Calming Measures Could be Considered

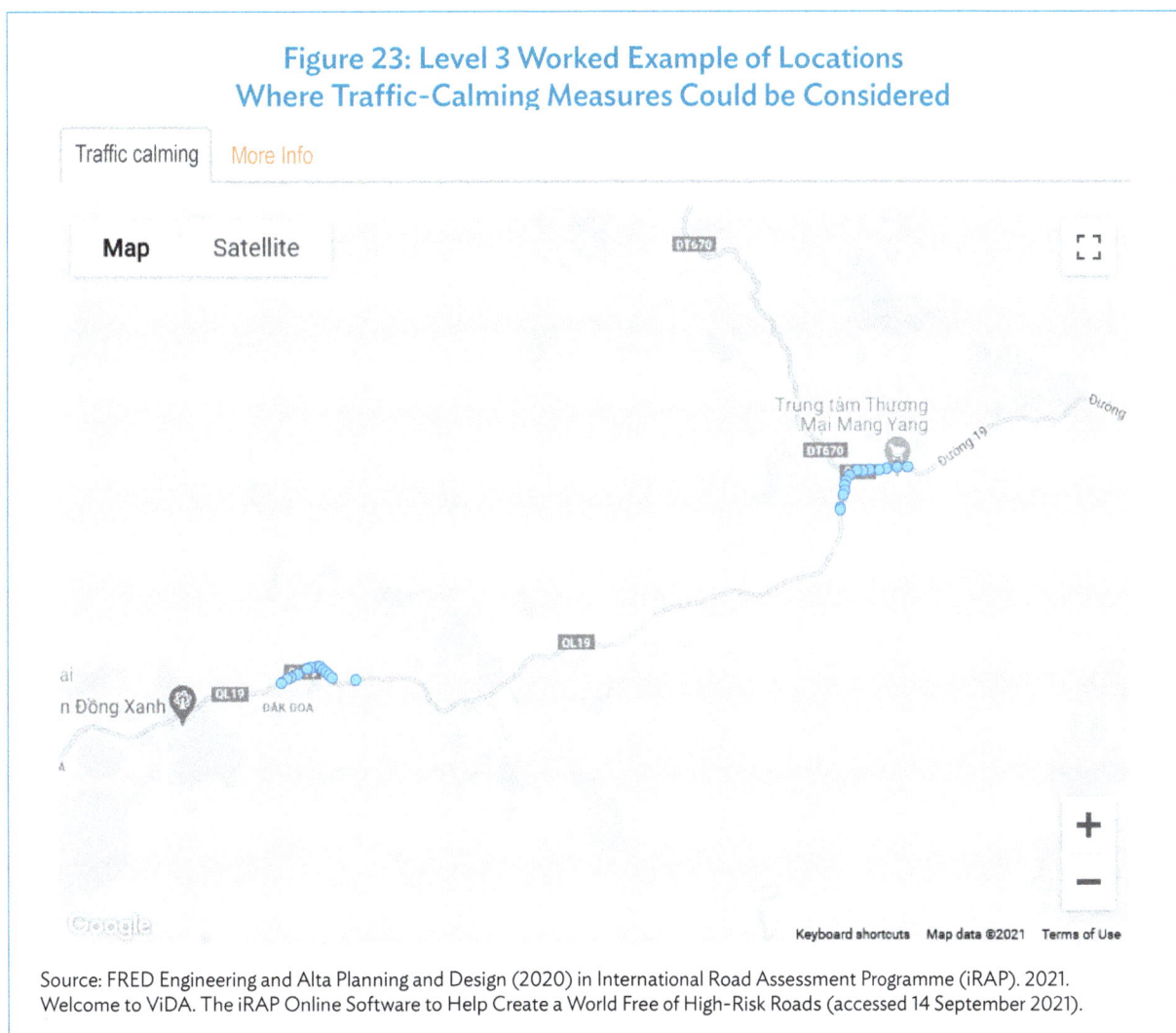

Source: FRED Engineering and Alta Planning and Design (2020) in International Road Assessment Programme (iRAP). 2021. Welcome to ViDA. The iRAP Online Software to Help Create a World Free of High-Risk Roads (accessed 14 September 2021).

Figure 24: Level 3 Worked Example of Locations Where Safety Barriers and/or Safe End Treatments Could be Considered

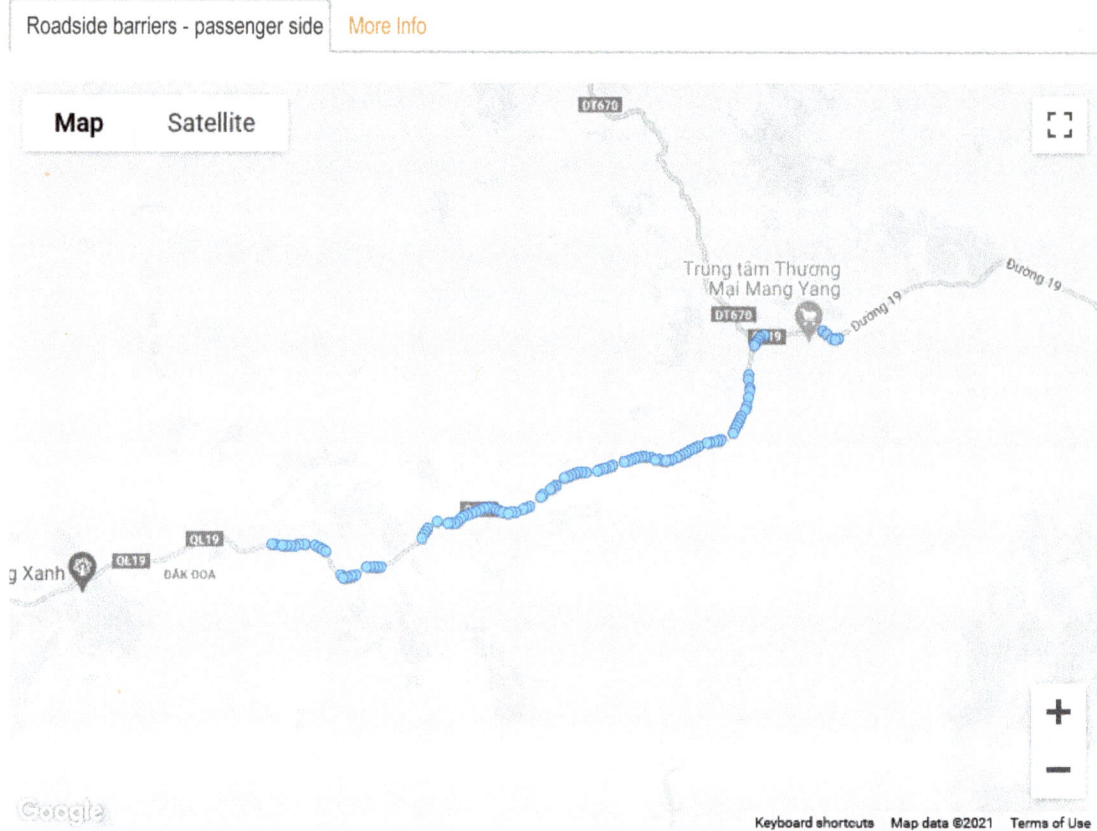

Source: FRED Engineering and Alta Planning and Design (2020) in International Road Assessment Programme. 2021 (iRAP). Welcome to ViDA. The iRAP Online Software to Help Create a World Free of High-Risk Roads (accessed 14 September 2021).

Figure 25: Level 3 Worked Example of Excerpt of a Strip Plan Listing Countermeasure Options along the Design

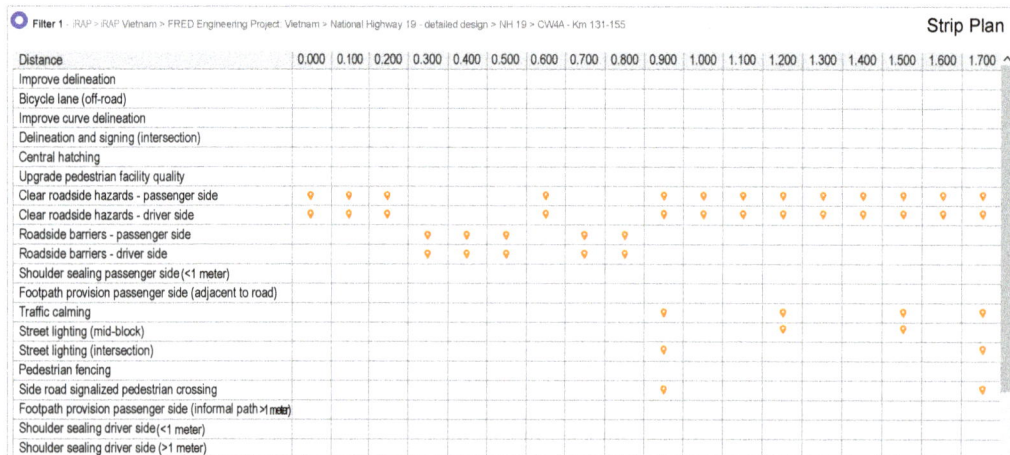

Filter 1 - iRAP > iRAP Vietnam > FRED Engineering Project: Vietnam > National Highway 19 - detailed design > NH 19 > CW4A - Km 131-155   Strip Plan

Distance	0.000	0.100	0.200	0.300	0.400	0.500	0.600	0.700	0.800	0.900	1.000	1.100	1.200	1.300	1.400	1.500	1.600	1.700
Improve delineation																		
Bicycle lane (off-road)																		
Improve curve delineation																		
Delineation and signing (intersection)																		
Central hatching																		
Upgrade pedestrian facility quality																		
Clear roadside hazards - passenger side	♀	♀	♀				♀			♀	♀	♀	♀	♀	♀	♀	♀	♀
Clear roadside hazards - driver side	♀	♀	♀				♀			♀	♀	♀	♀	♀	♀	♀	♀	♀
Roadside barriers - passenger side				♀	♀	♀		♀	♀									
Roadside barriers - driver side				♀	♀	♀		♀	♀									
Shoulder sealing passenger side (<1 meter)																		
Footpath provision passenger side (adjacent to road)																		
Traffic calming										♀			♀			♀		♀
Street lighting (mid-block)												♀				♀		
Street lighting (intersection)										♀								
Pedestrian fencing																		
Side road signalized pedestrian crossing										♀								♀
Footpath provision passenger side (informal path >1 meter)																		
Shoulder sealing driver side (<1 meter)																		
Shoulder sealing driver side (>1 meter)																		

Source: FRED Engineering and Alta Planning and Design (2020) in International Road Assessment Programme (iRAP). 2021. Welcome to ViDA. The iRAP Online Software to Help Create a World Free of High-Risk Roads (accessed 14 September 2021).

4. Level 3 Worked Example (Recommend Changes)

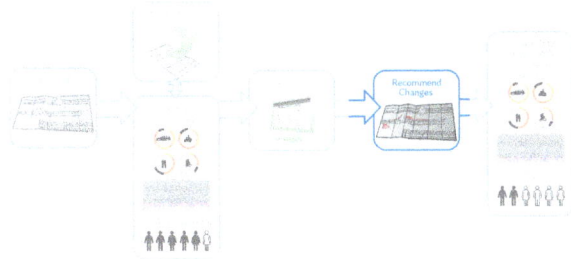

The audit team then developed recommendations addressing each safety concern. This included referencing the Star Ratings for the design, safety countermeasures options in the SRIP, the Road Safety Toolkit (https://toolkit.irap.org), and the Star Rating Demonstrator. Based on the experience of the audit team, their desktop review of the designs, and their site inspections, the audit team

could then determine whether the outputs from the SRIP were appropriate for the design.

The three safety concerns discussed earlier are shown in Figure 26, Figure 27, and Figure 28 along with the following recommendations made by the audit team:

(i) Replace the rigid concrete guideposts with frangible (breakable) guideposts. This raised the Star Ratings for vehicle occupants and motorcyclists from 2-Star to 3-Star.

(ii) Improve the stiffness of safety barriers that connect to bridge barriers. This raised the Star Ratings for vehicle occupants and motorcyclists from 2-Star to 3-Star.

(iii) Construct a sidewalk that can properly accommodate pedestrians in built-up areas. This raised the Star Ratings for pedestrians from 1-Star to 4-Star.

Figure 26: Level 3 Worked Example of Rigid Guidepost Safety Concern and Countermeasure

Ref	Safety Concern	Risk	Star Rating (Initial Design)	Recommendation	Star Rating (With Recommendation)	Client Response
3.3	A feature throughout the design (particularly in the 80 kph speed zone environments) and as part of the standard layout is the use of concrete guideposts. While the auditors support the addition of delineation features, the solid concrete posts present a runoff road hazard to an errant vehicle or motorcyclist. It is noted that the current design standards specific this post and foundation, however the auditors strongly recommend the client view this as a roadside hazard.	Medium	★★★☆☆ 17.72 / ★★★★☆ 19.54 / ★★★☆☆ 145.96 / ★★★★☆ 67.45	• Provide breakable guideposts throughout the route.	★★★☆☆ 9.8 / ★★★☆☆ 11.62 / ★★★☆☆ 145.96 / ★☆☆☆☆ 67.44	

kph = kilometers per hour.
Sources: International Road Assessment Programme (iRAP) and Safe System Solutions Pty Ltd.

Figure 27: Level 3 Worked Example of Safety Barrier Safety Concern and Countermeasure

Ref	Safety Concern	Risk	Star Rating (Initial Design)	Recommendation	Star Rating (With Recommendation)	Client Response
3.1	The transition between guardrail and bridge barrier is not adequate. In the last part of the guardrail there is no stiffening necessary for the transition to the bridge barrier. In the event of a collision, the guardrail would be more deformed than the bridge barrier, which would thus be a dangerous rigid obstacle. 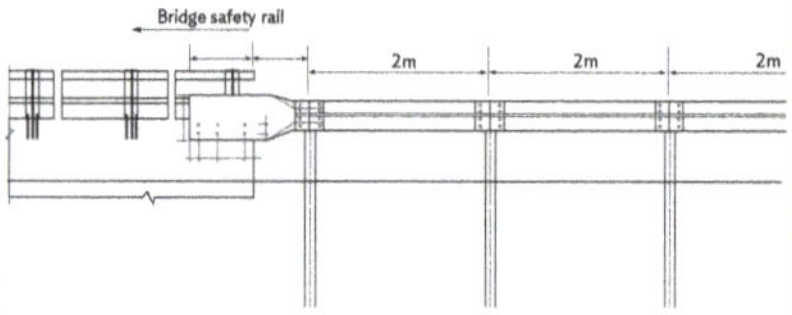	Medium	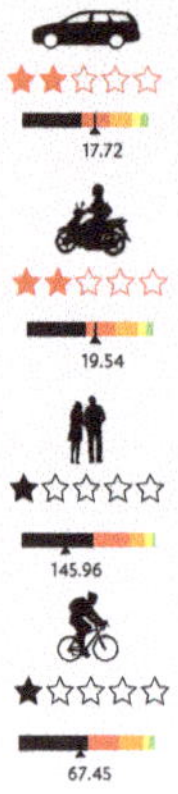 ★★☆☆☆ 17.72 / ★★☆☆☆ 19.54 / ★☆☆☆☆ 145.96 / ★☆☆☆☆ 67.45	• Ensure an appropriate transition between the two types of barriers to avoid performance changes. This can be achieved by progressive stiffening of the guardrail, for example by reducing the spacing of the posts. 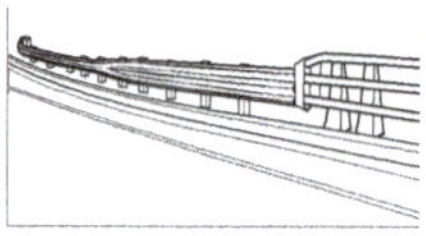	 ★★★☆☆ 6.45 / ★★★☆☆ 12.5 / ★☆☆☆☆ 145.96 / ★☆☆☆☆ 67.44	

Sources: International Road Assessment Programme (iRAP) and Safe System Solutions Pty Ltd.

Figure 28: Level 3 Worked Example of Sidewalk Safety Concern and Countermeasure

Ref	Safety Concern	Risk	Star Rating (Initial Design)	Recommendation	Star Rating (With Recommendation)	Client Response
1.7	Through densely populated areas, the flow of pedestrians is very high due to the presence of commercial activities, schools, residences, etc. Even if there is a covered ditch, the width of 1 meter is not enough to ensure the passage of pedestrians. If there is no sidewalk or if it is too narrow, pedestrians are forced to walk on the carriageway with the risk of being run over. The risk is higher during the rainy seasons, when possible informal footpaths may be muddy, discouraging pedestrians from using them. 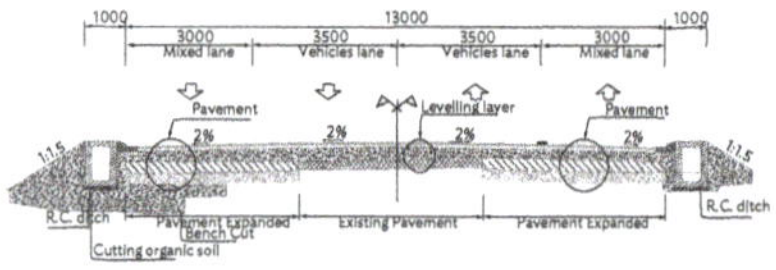	High	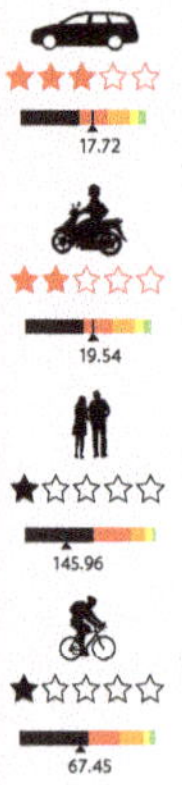 ★★★☆☆ 17.72 / ★★☆☆☆ 19.54 / ★☆☆☆☆ 145.96 / ★☆☆☆☆ 67.45	Provide a sidewalk along all built-up areas. In particular, the sidewalk must be separated from the roadway (with a reasonable kerb or barrier system) and should be offset by at least 3 meters with a path width of at least 2 meters wide.	 ★★☆☆☆ 17.72 / ★★☆☆☆ 19.54 / ★★★★☆ 0.32 / ★☆☆☆☆ 67.44	

Sources: International Road Assessment Programme (iRAP) and Safe System Solutions Pty Ltd.

5. Level 3 Worked Example (Star Rate Entire Design with Recommended Changes)

Prior to submitting the RSA report and recommendations, the audit team produced updated Star Ratings and fatality and serious injury estimates for the road design with their recommendations. The following results are presented and formed a compelling case:

(i)   Star Ratings improved for all road users and exceeded the target of 3-Star or better (Figure 29).

(ii)   There would be an overall 64% reduction in fatalities and serious injuries for all road users Figure 30).

Following receipt of the RSA report and recommendations, the client consulted the audit design team to decide on recommendations that they would accept. The accepted recommendations were then incorporated by the design team. The updated design was shared with the audit team for a final check and to ensure that all accepted recommendations were correctly adopted and documented in the design. A final SRS was performed to check the Star Rating of the agreed design.

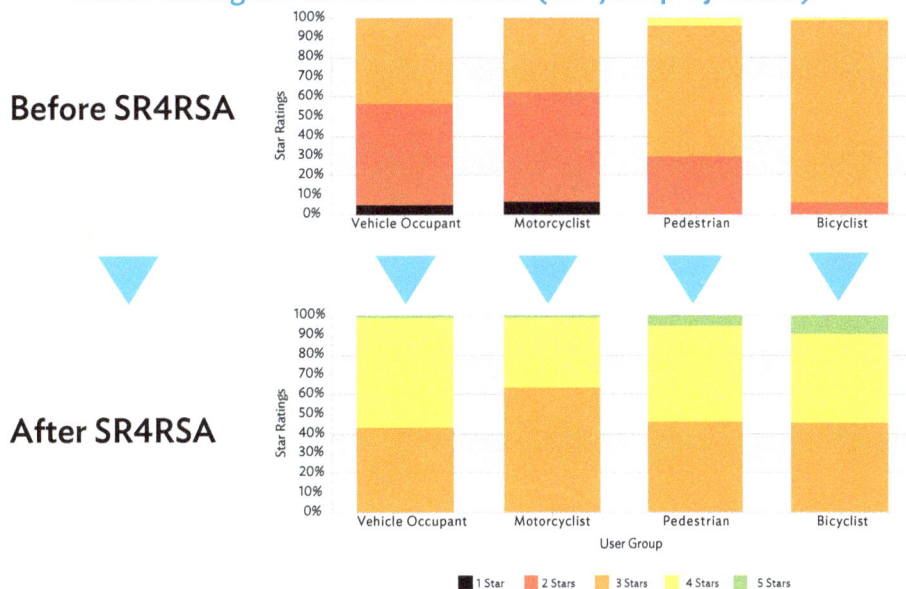

Figure 29: Level 3 Worked Example of Star Rating for the Design without Recommendations (top) and with Recommendations (bottom) Made during the SR4RSA Process (20-year project life)

SR4RSA = Star Rating for Road Safety Audit.
Note: 1-Star is highest risk and 5-Star is lowest risk.
Source: FRED Engineering and Alta Planning and Design. 2021. New Approach for a Comprehensive Road Safety Assessment Throughout the Entire Design Process. Presentation to the Technical Committee on 3.1 Road Safety at the Permanent International Association of Road Congresses International Seminar on Road Safety in Low- to Middle-Income Countries. 20 May 2021.

Figure 30: Level 3 Worked Example of Estimated Fatalities and Serious Injuries for the Design with and without Recommendations Made during the SR4RSA Process (20-year project life)

Initial Highway Upgrade Design (without SR4RSA recommendations)

Predicted Fatality and Serious Injuries:
Vehicle Occupants: 3.6   Motorcyclists: 22.8   Pedestrians: 2.7   Bicyclists: 6.2
TOTAL: 35.3

Altered Highway Upgrade Design (with SR4RSA recommendations)

Predicted Fatality and Serious Injuries:
Vehicle Occupants: 1.6   Motorcyclists: 9.8   Pedestrians: 1.4   Bicyclists: 2.2
TOTAL: 15.0
(58% reduction in Fatal and Serious Injuries)

SR4RSA = Star Rating for Road Safety Audit.
Sources: International Road Assessment Programme (iRAP) and Safe System Solutions Pty Ltd.

Situational scrutiny refers to the process of bringing RSA and engineering knowledge and experience to the coding of road attributes in the iRAP assessment. RSA thinking can assist in improving the quality of the iRAP coding inputs, and thus the quality of the outputs, helping ensure that the safety impacts of designs are understood and well communicated.

The SRS and Star Ratings are based on 52 design attributes, many of which have multiple coding options (the "Intersection Type" attribute, for example, has 17 options). The iRAP Coding Manual provides detailed instructions on how each attribute should be coded; nevertheless, the "coder" is often required to decide on the most appropriate coding option.

For example, for each attribute the coder is asked to select the "worst" case category within each 100 m segment. If a 100 m segment includes a cliff for 50 m and a safety barrier for the next 50 m, the coder records the cliff for the entire 100 m segment. For simple cases like this it is clear which is the "worst" case; however, in other coding situations some advanced judgment is required. This is one of the situations where a road safety auditor's expert judgment can assist in improving the accuracy of the Star Rating process. This situational is also an example of where the iRAP methodology may underestimate the safety impact of parts of a design. In this case, by applying the worst-case category to the whole 100 m segment, the benefit of the safety barrier that spans 50 m is not able to be reflected in the Star Ratings.

Another aspect in which a road safety auditor's expert judgment is beneficial is when the specific situation cannot be coded. An example is pedestrian fencing that performs well in reducing risk in most situations, but in some specific scenarios it may do the opposite and increases risk. The only option in the iRAP methodology is to code it as pedestrian fencing that reduces the risk, and it is therefore necessary for the auditor to provide additional information to explain the potential risks.

In some situations, there are road safety attributes that do not have coding options within iRAP, such as increasing retro reflectivity, rest areas for trucks, pram

ramps, superelevation, and drainage. The Star Rating cannot reflect these features (or lack of features) and requires an expert to review the design or existing road to understand and communicate the impact on road safety that is not fully captured in the iRAP results.

In some instances, road designs do not contain all road attributes needed for an iRAP assessment. This is not unusual for concept designs but also can be the case for detailed designs. Based on their knowledge of a situation, an experienced road safety auditor is likely to be able to make good judgments about the attributes that are likely to be present and communicate the assumptions underpinning their reasoning.

The following are examples of where situational context change the Star Rating or the expected road safety outcome has been influenced by the specifics of the situation and the Star Rating may not fully reflect that specific scenario.

A.   Example 1: Pedestrian Bridge for Rehabilitated Road

Grade separated facility

Code: 1

A physically separated pedestrian crossing that does not bring pedestrians into conflict with road traffic flows. May include pedestrian overbridges or underpasses (subways).

Do note code grade separated facilities if pedestrians cross at street level.

When coding a pedestrian facility in iRAP, there is a binary choice to be made by the coder: Will the pedestrian facility be fully effective or not? The coder could make a judgment based on their knowledge of the area or their expectation, but an experienced road safety auditor will be able to make more informed and specific judgments based on their knowledge of the land use, pedestrian desired lines, cultural nuances, facility design, perceptions of personal safety using the facility, road user preferences, and other situation-specific inputs.

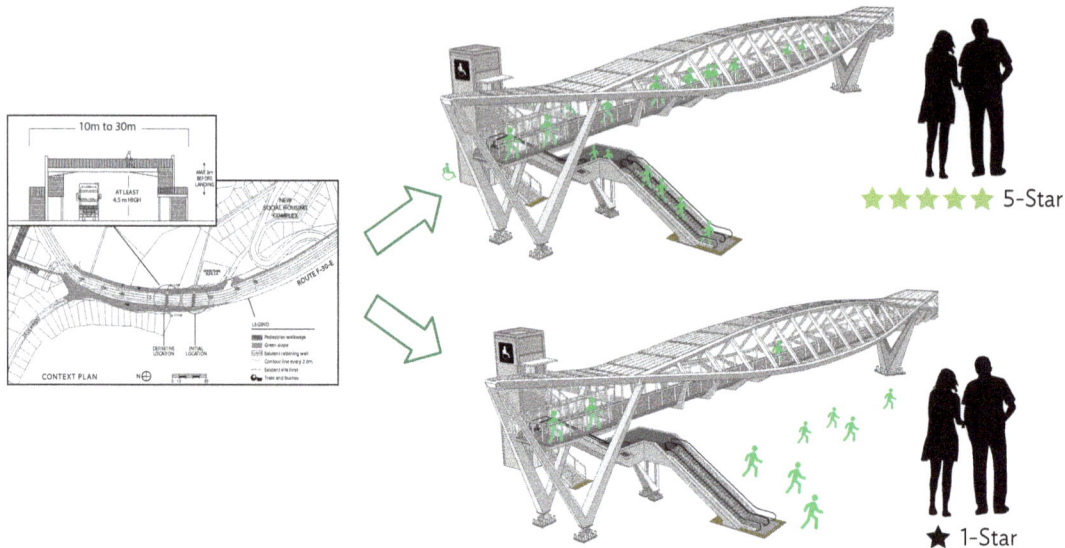

Figure 31: Situational Scrutiny Can Help Star Rate a Pedestrian Bridge

Note: 1-Star is highest risk and 5-Star is lowest risk.
Sources: International Road Assessment Programme (iRAP) and Safe System Solutions Pty Ltd.

While a design may contain a pedestrian overpass facility, the pedestrian SRS can be dramatically different based on the specific situation. Figure 31 shows a road design where a pedestrian overpass is planned. The Star Rating for that section of the highway could either be 5-Star or 1-Star for pedestrians based on the behavior of people walking in the area and presence (or lack of) complementary infrastructure. An experienced road safety auditor can understand and communicate the risk associated with the situation.

B.   Example 2: Safety Barrier End Terminals

Another example of the specific situation influencing the SRS is the choice of coding for a safety barrier end terminal. When coding this road feature, the coder must decide if the barrier end terminal should be classified as "unprotected safety barrier end" or not. The iRAP Coding Manual provides guidance and lists ramped ends, unprotected ends, sharp ends, or fish-tail terminals as being hazardous (or unprotected). However, detailed knowledge of safety barrier end terminals is required to understand the variety of barrier end terminals and if they should be categorized in this fashion, or if they are appropriate. An experienced road safety auditor can provide specific detailed input to determine the safety benefit or risk presented by the end terminal.

Figure 32 illustrates examples of different end terminals available worldwide. Some of these would be coded as "unprotected safety barrier end" and some would be a protected barrier end and coded as such.

C.   Example 3: Pedestrian Fencing

Pedestrian fencing has two coding options in the iRAP methodology: present and not present. If a road design includes pedestrian fencing, the SRS for pedestrians improves as it implies that pedestrians will not cross the road at that location. However, in some situations a pedestrian fence can trap pedestrians on the road thereby increasing the risk of a pedestrian being struck (Figure 33). This risk cannot be coded in the iRAP methodology and requires the situational scrutiny of an experienced road safety auditor to understand and communicate the risk. This is an example of where the risk rating produced by the road safety auditor will be able to clearly reflect the specific situation.

Figure 32: Situational Scrutiny Can Help Star Rate a Safety Barrier End Terminal

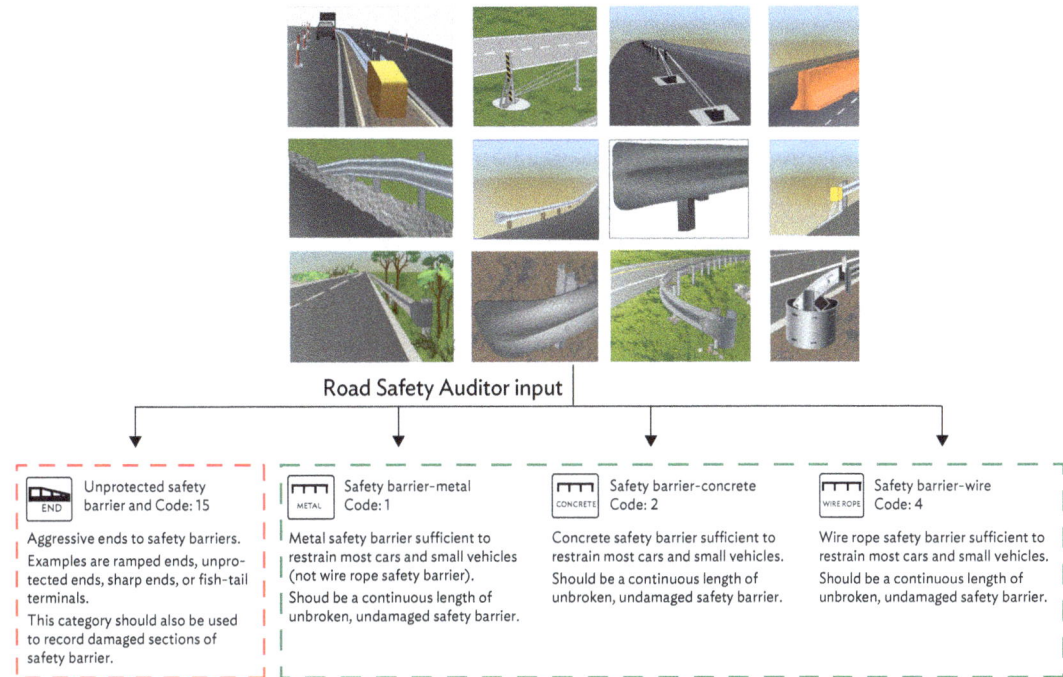

Road Safety Auditor input

Unprotected safety barrier and Code: 15

Aggressive ends to safety barriers. Examples are ramped ends, unprotected ends, sharp ends, or fish-tail terminals.

This category should also be used to record damaged sections of safety barrier.

Safety barrier-metal Code: 1

Metal safety barrier sufficient to restrain most cars and small vehicles (not wire rope safety barrier).

Shoud be a continuous length of unbroken, undamaged safety barrier.

Safety barrier-concrete Code: 2

Concrete safety barrier sufficient to restrain most cars and small vehicles.

Should be a continuous length of unbroken, undamaged safety barrier.

Safety barrier-wire Code: 4

Wire rope safety barrier sufficient to restrain most cars and small vehicles.

Should be a continuous length of unbroken, undamaged safety barrier.

Sources: International Road Assessment Programme (iRAP) and Safe System Solutions Pty Ltd.

Figure 33: Pedestrians "Trapped" on the Roadway by the Pedestrian Fence

iRAP Coding Options

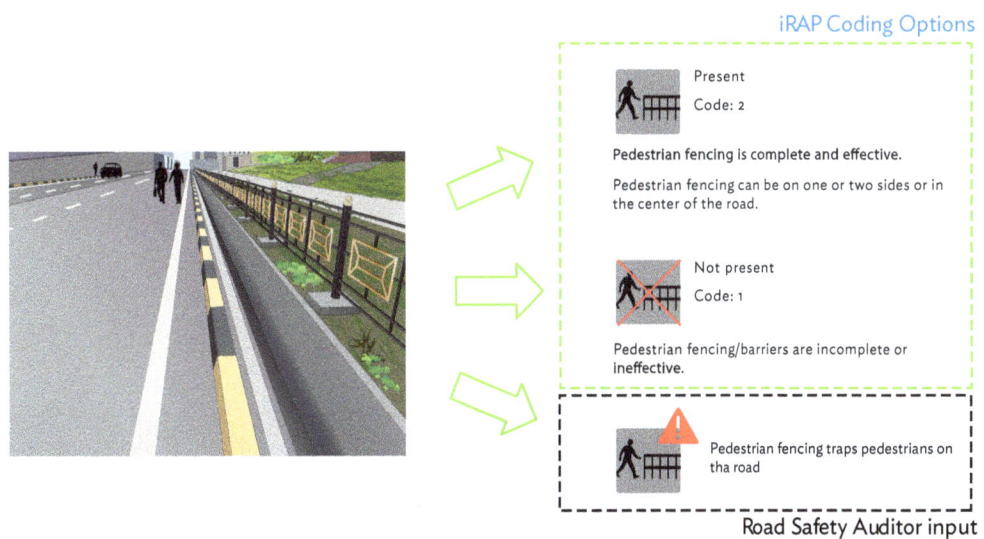

Present Code: 2

Pedestrian fencing is complete and effective.

Pedestrian fencing can be on one or two sides or in the center of the road.

Not present Code: 1

Pedestrian fencing/barriers are incomplete or ineffective.

Pedestrian fencing traps pedestrians on tha road

Road Safety Auditor input

Sources: International Road Assessment Programme (iRAP), Safe System Solutions Pty Ltd, and Matt Chamberlain.

Other situation-specific questions an experienced road safety auditor may ask about the presence of a pedestrian fence in a design could be as follows:

(i)   Could the proposed fencing obstruct a driver or rider's view of pedestrians on the footpath or those about to cross the road? If so, it may be coded as creating poor sight distance.
(ii)   Could the fence be a potential spearing or snagging hazard for an errant driver or rider? If so, it may be coded as a roadside hazard.
(iii) If breaks in the fence are created for crossing points, do they align with pedestrians' desired lines (i.e., the direct path between a pedestrian's origin and destination)? If not, pedestrians are more likely to climb or jump over the fence rather than walk along the road's side of the fence.
(iv)   Is there access for all pedestrians including those who are mobility-impaired?
(v)   Has the proposed fencing considered animals on the road including those crossing from adjacent forests or fields? Will the fence trap animals on the road thus creating a road safety risk?
(vi)   Is there sufficient offset from the travel lane to minimize nuisance hits?

(vii) Does the new fence impact passengers alighting public transport?
(viii) Could the pedestrian fencing result in tunnel vision leading to increased speeds?

D.   Example 4: Line Marking

Delineation (e.g., line markings, signs, and reflectors) has two coding options in iRAP: poor and adequate. Road designs are likely to improve the line marking and delineation thus the delineation is likely to be coded as adequate. However, in some situations, the line marking, signs, or reflectors can add risk. For example, they can direct drivers into hazardous situations. This situation cannot be coded in the iRAP methodology and requires situational scrutiny by the road safety auditor. This is another example where the road safety auditor's risk rating is the mechanism to present the situational risk as the iRAP methodology will not reflect this.

In the example below (Figure 34) the line marking is clear and visible. The center lane directs road users to either continue along a straight travel line or to turn right. However, it is only the right lane that exists to the off-ramp. In this situation, vehicles traveling in the center lane are at an increased risk of either crashing

Figure 34: Pavement Arrows Creating a Potential Conflict for Vehicles in the Center Lane

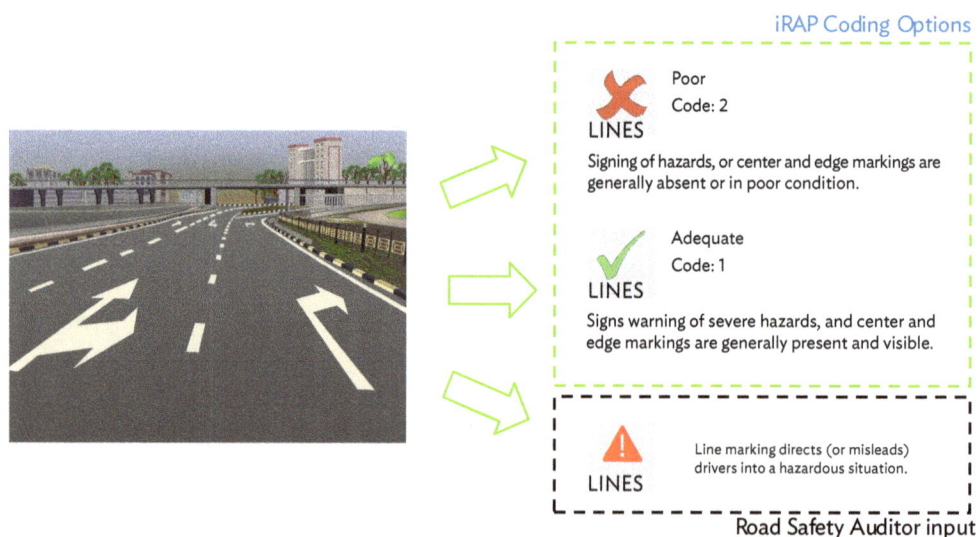

Sources: International Road Assessment Programme (iRAP), Safe System Solutions Pty Ltd., and Matt Chamberlain.

into the roadside gorge area or into vehicles traveling in the right lane.

An experienced road safety auditor may ask other situation-specific questions about the delineation in a design:

(i)   Could the line marking confuse a driver or rider?
(ii)   Could the signs or combination of signs confuse a driver or rider?
(iii)   Will the delineation be sufficiently retroreflective at night?
(iv)   Will the signs block paths for pedestrians or cyclists?
(v)   Are the new signs a strike hazard for motorcyclists or cyclists?
(vi)   Do the new signs block sightlines at intersections or access points?
(vii)   Will the line marking be a slip hazard for pedestrians, cyclists, or motorcyclists?
(viii) Are the correct signs being used?

E.   Example 5: Speed

The level of risk of death or serious injury on a road is highly dependent on the speed at which traffic travels.

Star Ratings are based on the *greater* of the speed limit and the 85th percentile speed. The 85th percentile speed is often provided to the team by the road controlling authority that has collected that data, or data is collected during site inspections.

Information on the 85th percentile vehicle travel speed cannot be collected if a road is yet to be built or the alterations are yet to be made. Thus, an estimate of the operating travel speed is required as an input for the iRAP Star Rating coding. The coder may estimate the 85th percentile vehicle travel speed based on data collected from a similar and existing road, their knowledge of the area, or their experience. However, an experienced road safety auditor will be able to make an informed and specific judgment based on their experience with similar designs, knowledge on driving and/or riding behavior in the area, expected enforcement levels, and other situation-specific parameters.

Figure 35 indicates a road that has been constructed and is about to be open to the public. The speed limit (permanent) has been posted at 100 kph; however, the audit team estimates that the operating speed is likely to be closer to 120 kph. Thus, 120 kph will be used when calculating the SRS for the road.

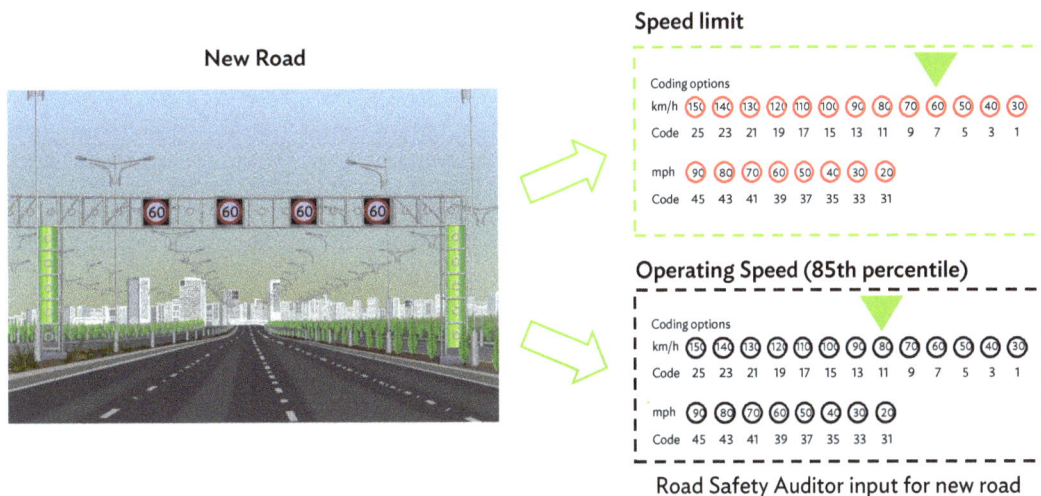

Figure 35: Operating Speeds May Be Higher than Design Speeds or Posted Speed Limit

New Road

Speed limit

Coding options
km/h 150 140 130 120 110 100 90 80 70 60 50 40 30
Code   25   23   21   19   17   15 13 11   9   7   5   3   1

mph   90 80 70 60 50 40 30 20
Code 45 43 41 39 37 35 33 31

Operating Speed (85th percentile)

Coding options
km/h 150 140 130 120 110 100 90 80 70 60 50 40 30
Code   25   23   21   19   17   15 13 11   9   7   5   3   1

mph   90 80 70 60 50 40 30 20
Code 45 43 41 39 37 35 33 31

Road Safety Auditor input for new road

km/h = kilometers per hour, mph = miles per hour.
Sources: International Road Assessment Programme (iRAP), Safe System Solutions Pty Ltd., and Asian Development Bank.

F.   Example 6: Details in Designs Are Missing

In some instances, road designs do not contain all road attributes needed for an iRAP assessment. This is not unusual for concept designs but can also be the case for detailed designs. For example, cross-section drawings might indicate standard roadside features but not include specific details such as trees, property access points, and culverts. In these cases, two options are generally available for the iRAP road attribute coding:

(i)   **Assume the existing road design details will continue onto the new road.** For example, if an existing road that is being upgraded currently has poles along the median but the upgraded design documents do not specify pole locations, then it may be assumed that poles will be installed in the median (Figure 36). The information on where the poles are to be located for the upgraded road may be available in an iRAP assessment that has previously been performed for an existing road, or obtained from photos of the existing road, or collected during audit site inspections.

(ii)   **Reasonable assumptions if photos or other documentation of the current road situation are not available.** An experienced road safety auditor may select an attribute based on a reasonable assumption of what is likely to be present. Assumptions made during the assessment would occur in consultation with the client and design team and should be well documented. Further, assumptions should be as consistent as possible throughout the assessment.

Due to the level of detail required by the iRAP methodology, there are many situations that require expert judgment of the proposed design. The above examples have been presented to demonstrate where situational scrutiny is required. Experienced road safety auditors can provide this fine level of design detail assumption and contextualize the design for a particular situation, i.e., they can provide necessary situational scrutiny.

Figure 36: Example Showing a Cross Section for Upgrade and Image of Road to Be Upgraded

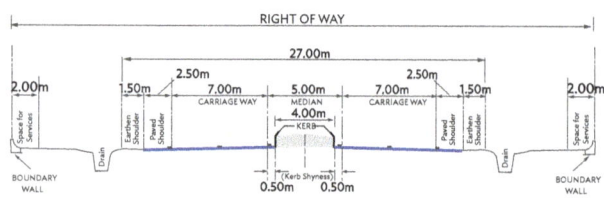

TYPICAL CROSS SECTION TYPE A-3
(Open Country Plain/Rolling Terrain)

Four-Lane Divided Highway without Service Roads and with Raised Median

Note: The illustration on the left shows a cross section for upgrade. The image on the right shows a road to be upgraded.
Sources: Indian Road Congress (IRC). 2019. *IRC:SP:84-2019 Manual of Specifications and Standards for Four Laning of Highways*. New Delhi; and J. Bhavsar. 2021. *IndiaRAP Safety Assessment of National Highway Network in Uttar Pradesh, Maharashtra, and Tamil Nadu*. India.

XI.   Engaging with Stakeholders

The concept of situational scrutiny relies on one of the most significant characteristics of good auditors, which is their ability to put themselves in the shoes of future road users. Engaging with stakeholders in a road project is an effective way of achieving this. Meaningful participation of a range of stakeholders in decision-making and implementation of road projects can accelerate progress and help ensure that designs facilitate safe and efficient journeys for everyone.

Although it is not the role of the audit team to develop and implement a stakeholder engagement plan for road project (this is a role for the client), it is important that the SR4RSA process is performed in conjunction with such an engagement process.

While reviewing design documentation, the audit team should also review data and reports produced from stakeholder engagement activities performed as part of the project planning process. When data and reports are not available, the audit team can,

for example, carry out a more in-depth situational analysis as part of site inspections in areas where vulnerable road users are likely to be present. Touching base with road user groups of particular concern (e.g., farmers and schoolteachers), and participating in stakeholder engagement activities, such as workshops or community meetings, is also worthwhile.

It is helpful if the audit team is composed of members with a diverse background and local experience, particularly of differing skill sets, ages, and genders. Working with local partners with a knowledge of the community is also beneficial.

This approach can increase the likelihood that the most significant potential safety concerns and effective recommendations are identified.

XII. Collecting Data during Site Inspections

An inspection of the location of the new design is a standard part of an RSA as described in the *CAREC RSE Manual 1* and are an important part of the situational scrutiny process. Site inspections are also an opportunity to gather data that can be used with the iRAP methodology. As such, when planning a site inspection, consideration should be given to the collection of data that can be used for the iRAP methodology. The data are described in Table 4.

The *iRAP Survey Manual* and *Star Rating and Investment Plan Manual* provide further guidance on how these data can be collected and how the data are used.[26]

Table 4: Data That Can Be Collected during a Site Inspection for Use with the International Road Audit Programme Methodology

Data Type	Rationale
Traffic speeds	• The speed of traffic is fundamental to road safety. • iRAP Star Ratings are based on the greater of the posted speed limit or the estimated 85th percentile speed.
Traffic counts	• The volume of motorized vehicles using a road affects both risk and the likelihood of deaths and serious injuries. • Star Ratings, fatality estimations, and investment plans require vehicle volume estimates.
Pedestrian flow counts	• To document pedestrian "desired lines." • Star Ratings, fatality estimations, and investment plans for pedestrians require pedestrian volume estimates.
Bicyclist flow counts	• To document bicyclist "desired lines." • Star Ratings, fatality estimations, and investment plans for bicyclists require bicyclist volume estimates.
Road attributes	• In some instances, road design documents do not contain all road attributes needed by the iRAP methodology. These data may be collected during site inspections.

iRAP = International Road Assessment Programme.
Sources: iRAP and Safe System Solutions Pty Ltd.

26 iRAP. 2021. iRAP Specification, Manuals and Guides (accessed 14 September 2021).

As discussed in Chapter 4, the iRAP methodology may be used in road safety inspections on existing roads. It is possible to combine the results of such an inspection with a Level 1, 2, or 3 SR4RSA. The inspections can be performed before the design process begins to provide a baseline set of metrics, and after the designs are constructed to confirm the road complies with the targets set in the design.

There are several benefits in this:

(i)   The findings from the inspection can be used for planning road investment priorities and incorporated in design concepts at the earliest stages thus minimizing the need for redesigns latter in the process.

(ii) Targets that reflect the existing situation can be set at an early stage.

(iii) A baseline Star Rating can be established and improvements relative to this baseline can be easily tracked from design through to construction completion.

Figure 37 illustrates the relationships for the Level 1, 2, and 3 SR4RSA processes.

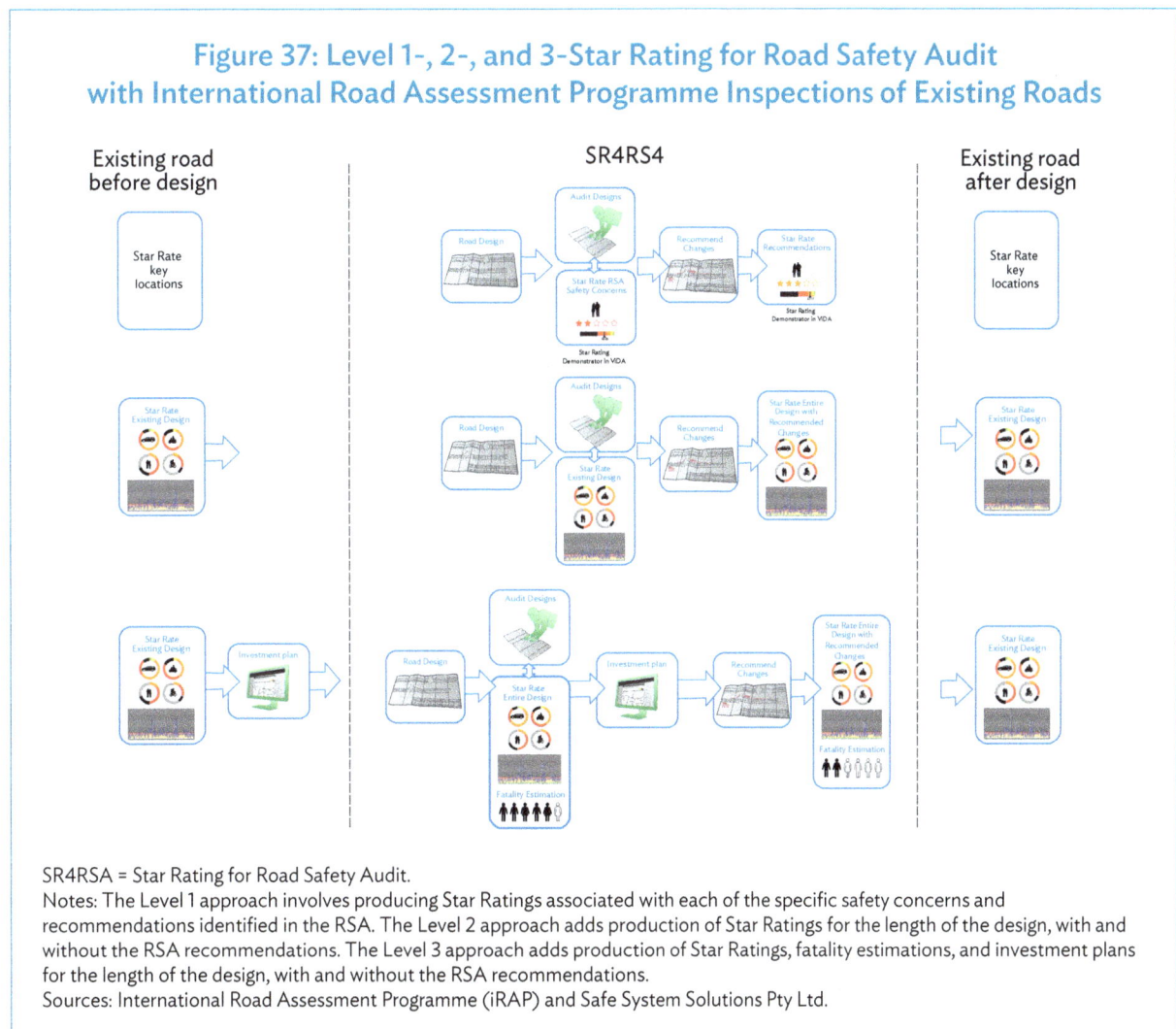

Figure 37: Level 1-, 2-, and 3-Star Rating for Road Safety Audit with International Road Assessment Programme Inspections of Existing Roads

SR4RSA = Star Rating for Road Safety Audit.
Notes: The Level 1 approach involves producing Star Ratings associated with each of the specific safety concerns and recommendations identified in the RSA. The Level 2 approach adds production of Star Ratings for the length of the design, with and without the RSA recommendations. The Level 3 approach adds production of Star Ratings, fatality estimations, and investment plans for the length of the design, with and without the RSA recommendations.
Sources: International Road Assessment Programme (iRAP) and Safe System Solutions Pty Ltd.

XIV. Training and Competencies

While RSA and iRAP are processes that are free and accessible, they each require specialist skills and knowledge. Table 5 summarizes the recommended training and competencies for those performing SR4RSA in a design project.

Courses for RSA vary from region to region, but generally comprise 1–2 weeks of training and fieldwork. The Star Rating for Designs (SR4D) courses comprises 4 x 1.5-hour online modules plus assignments.[27] An SR4RSA fundamentals course typically comprises 2 x 1.5-hour modules online plus assignments.

In addition to the training and competencies for the audit team, it is desirable that the client and design team also develop knowledge and skills in the iRAP methodology. This ensures that they can understand results and recommendations from an SR4RSA report and therefore make informed decisions. This will also enable design teams to perform Star Rating checks of their own designs as they are developed.

iRAP also manages an accreditation scheme. iRAP accreditation is for individuals and is awarded based on completion of training, passing an accreditation test, signing of a code of conduct, and demonstrated experience in delivering assessment activities. It is beneficial that those performing iRAP assessments, particularly design teams and audit teams, hold iRAP accreditation though it is not mandatory. It is also desirable that key client technical staff gain iRAP accreditation so that they can fully engage with the audit and design teams on the iRAP assessment process and results.[28]

Table 5: Recommended Training and Competencies for SR4RSA

Training and Competencies	SR4RSA Level		
	Level 1	Level 2	Level 3
Road Safety Audit Training and Competencies			
Completion of a formal road safety audit course	✓	✓	✓
Experience as a road safety auditor	✓	✓	✓
International Road Audit Program Training and Competencies			
Ability to use the Star Rating Demonstrator	✓	✓	✓
Completion of SR4D course		✓	✓
Ability to use the SR4D tool		✓	✓
SR4RSA Competency			
Completion of an SR4RSA fundamentals course	✓	✓	✓

SR4D = Star Rating for Designs, SR4RSA = Star Rating for Road Safety Audit.
Sources: International Road Assessment Programme (iRAP) and Safe System Solutions Pty Ltd.

---

27   iRAP. 2021. *Training* (accessed 14 September 2021).
28   iRAP. 2021. *Accreditation* (accessed 14 September 2021).

This sample terms of reference are adapted from the *CAREC Road Safety Engineering Manual 1*.

TERMS OF REFERENCE FOR A [insert stage name] STAGE STAR RATINGS FOR ROAD SAFETY AUDIT (SR4RSA) OF [insert name of the road project]

Background

The *[insert name of road authority]* has developed a proposal to *[insert a brief description of the type and location of the proposal]* to provide improved capacity and traffic performance along this corridor as well as increased safety for all road users.

The Task

The task in this assignment is to carry out a *[insert stage name]* stage Star Rating for Road Safety Audit (SR4RSA) of the proposed *[insert name of project]* so potential road safety problems can be identified, discussed, and minimized before the project is completed.

A Level *{insert 1, 2 or 3}* SR4RSA shall be undertaken in accordance with *{name of national road safety legislation, strategy, action plan}* and the process detailed in the current edition of the *CAREC Road Safety Engineering Manual 5*, and *CAREC Road Safety Engineering Manual 1*.

Scope of Services

The scope of services required of the audit team will include, but is not necessarily limited to, the following:

- The audit should be undertaken by an audit team of at least two auditors.
- The team leader should be a registered senior road safety auditor in at least one national register of road safety auditors.
- The team shall include at least one member that holds iRAP Accreditation in analysis and reporting.
- The team leader should attend a commencement meeting with the project manager and designer to obtain full information about the proposal and an understanding of the background to the project.
- Documents provided by the project manager prior to inspecting the site and again prior to finalizing the audit report should be reviewed.
- Daytime and nighttime inspections should be undertaken of the entire site to provide a better understanding of the existing traffic situation and an insight into how the finished project will look. Samples of traffic speeds should be collected during the site inspections.
- The auditors should consult the appropriate checklist in the CAREC Road Safety Audit Manual, but they should not limit their audit to the concerns listed therein. They shall look at the safety needs of all future road users of this location, especially vulnerable road users.
- A concise road safety audit report should be prepared in the format outlined in the current edition of the CAREC Road Safety Engineering Manuals 1 and 5.
- The audit report should include a clear description of all safety issues identified. It should contain practical recommendations for each safety issue of an appropriate and specific nature.
- The audit report should include Star Ratings and Star rating scores (SRS) for vehicle occupants, motorcyclists, pedestrians, and bicyclists for each safety issue identified and recommendation made, as outlined in the current edition of the *CAREC Road Safety Engineering Manual 5*.

- The team leader should sign and send the audit report electronically to the project manager.
- The team leader should attend the project manager's completion meeting to answer questions about the audit findings, the audit recommendations, and to discuss possible design changes.

The following information will be made available by the road authority to the audit team leader: *[insert the list of reports, drawings, data, photographs, previous iRAP methodology reports or other background information.]*

Qualifications and Experience

The audit services are to be provided by a team comprising two or more road safety engineering specialists; at least one (the team leader) should be a registered senior road safety auditor in a national register of accredited road safety auditors. At least one member should hold iRAP Accreditation in analysis and reporting. The audit team requires sound knowledge of road safety engineering and practical experience in highway design and traffic engineering.

Required Inputs *[Adjust these requirements to suit the scale and complexity of the project]*
The assignment is expected to take up to .... person-days, as follows:
_____ person-days for reviewing the reports and/or drawings and attending the commencement meeting
_____ person-days for inspecting the site (daytime and nighttime inspections are required)
_____ person-days for preparing the road safety audit report

Reporting

The senior road safety auditor should submit the completed and signed road safety audit report to the project manager in electronic format by *[write submission date for the audit report].*

Any questions about the proposal or the audit are to be directed by the senior auditor to *[insert name of the responsible engineer] via telephone [insert number] or e-mail [insert e-mail address].*

Source: Adapted from: ADB. 2018. *CAREC Road Safety Engineering Manual 1: Road Safety Audit.* Manila.

Glossary

Black spot investigation – a review of a road length or intersection with a crash history (a high-risk location). The review entails detailed investigation into the crash circumstances.

Crash rate risk – the mapping of historical reported crash data and associated road length and traffic flow data to show the statistical risk of death or serious injury. Crash risk maps are often used to show either crash rate, i.e., the relative risk to an individual road user (crashes per vehicle kilometer traveled), or crash density/collective risk, i.e., to the community as a whole (crashes per kilometer).

Star Rating and Star Rating Scores (SRS) – an assessment of risk on an existing road or road design using the International Road Assessment Programme (iRAP) Star Rating methodology and is normally combined with the iRAP Safer Road Investment Plan methodology. 1-Star roads have the highest level of risk of death and serious injury, and 5-star roads have the lowest level of risk of death and serious injury. Star rating scores (SRS) are a unitless decimal number underpin the Star Ratings.

Road safety audit – an independent, detailed, systematic, and technical safety check relating to the design characteristics of a road infrastructure project and covering all stages from planning to early operation. Road safety audits are qualitative in nature.

Road safety impact assessment – a strategic comparative analysis of the impact of a new road or a substantial modification to the existing network on the safety performance of the road network.

Road safety inspection (periodic) – a periodical verification of the characteristics and defects that require maintenance work for reasons of safety.

Road safety inspection (targeted) – a targeted investigation to identify hazardous conditions, defects, and problems that increase the risk of crashes, based on a site visit of an existing road or section of road. In some countries this is referred to as a road safety check, road safety diagnostic, or an existing conditions road safety audit.

Safe System assessment – a holistic risk evaluation methodology that quantifies alignment with Safe System principles. It includes an assessment of exposure, and likelihood and severity of crashes, including a review of the road and roadside, speeds, people, vehicles, and post-crash response.

Safety rating – the classification of parts of an existing road network into categories according to their objectively measured built-in safety. This is often done using the iRAP methodology.

Global Road Safety Performance Targets – a set of 12 voluntary actions agreed upon by United Nations Member States under the Decade of Action for Road Safety 2021–2030 (the Global Plan).

www.ingramcontent.com/pod-product-compliance
Lightning Source LLC
Chambersburg PA
CBHW050052220326
41599CB00045B/7375